"WHY DON'T THEY LEARN ENGLISH?"

Separating Fact from Fallacy in the U.S. Language Debate

Lucy Tse

Teachers College, Columbia University
New York and London

To Jane Gee and Yin Yui Tse, who inspire me more than they know

Published by Teachers College Press, 1234 Amsterdam Avenue, New York, NY 10027

Library of Congress Cataloging-in-Publication Data

Tse, Lucy.
   "Why don't they learn English?": Separating fact from fallacy in the U.S. language debate / Lucy Tse.
      p. cm. — (Language and literacy series)
   Includes bibliographical references and index.
   ISBN 0-8077-4097-7 (acid-free paper) — ISBN 0-8077-4096-9 (pbk. : acid-free paper)
     1. Language policy—United States. 2. English language—Study and teaching—Foreign speakers. 3. English language—Study and teaching—United States. 4. Immigrants—United States—Language. 5. Bilingualism—United States. I. Title. II. Language and literacy series (New York, N.Y.)

   P119.32.U6 T78 2001
   306.44'973—dc21   2001027750

ISBN 0-8077-4096-9 (paper)
ISBN 0-8077-4097-7 (cloth)

Printed on acid-free paper

Manufactured in the United States of America

08 07 06 05 04 03 02 01   8 7 6 5 4 3 2 1

Contents

Introduction

My purpose in writing this book is to address two important language-related issues: the often-made claim that immigrants don't learn English, and the common assumption that immigrants cling to their home language and perpetuate it from one generation to another. This book is intended to provide a short, readable introduction on these issues for the nonspecialist, but one that is well supported by research. For that reason, I have written the volume for those with limited previous experience in these topics, while including endnotes that provide academic references, further description of studies, and expansion and further discussions appropriate for the more experienced reader.

We are surrounded in the United States by economic, political, and educational debates involving language that have important and far-reaching implications. Bilingual education, English as the official language, and immigration are only a few of the hot-button issues that have divided public opinion. Whether immigrants are learning English and preserving the immigrant language are at the core of many of these controversies. In this book, I have attempted to provide an accurate picture of the state of English and immigrant languages in the United States, with the hope of making a small contribution toward shaping public perception on these important policy issues.

In this book I focus on English- and immigrant language issues by addressing the following questions:

- Chapter 1: What are the major claims made about immigrants and their English language learning? How widespread are these assumptions and how do they affect public policy?
- Chapter 2: Are immigrants learning English and do they resist doing so? Are the children of immigrants learning English and succeeding academically in school?

- Chapter 3: Are immigrant languages being perpetuated from one generation to another? What language is favored by immigrant children?
- Chapter 4: What are the consequences of developing or not developing immigrant languages for immigrant children and larger society? What programs are currently available to teach immigrant languages?
- Chapter 5: What factors promote language learning? What methods are effective in developing immigrant languages?

In the last chapter, Chapter 6, I summarize the previous chapters and suggest directions for educational policy.

My aim in writing this book and its necessarily short length have resulted in the omission or only cursory treatment of many important related topics. For instance, language loss among indigenous populations is mentioned only briefly, since although there are similarities between the immigrant and indigenous language experiences in the United States, there are equally important differences that this slim volume does not allow me to explore thoroughly. Readers interested in these issues are encouraged to consult the works of Teresa McCarty, Kathryn Au, and John Reyner, to name just a few who have made important contributions to this area of study.

Also absent is a substantive discussion of the power dynamics that underlie all language issues. Although I do mention the importance of power relations in the endnotes of several chapters, again this topic could not be treated with the depth it deserves. For those interested in further reading, I recommend the influential writings of Paulo Freire, Henry Giroux, Robert Phillipson, and Pierre Bourdieu, among others.

A third area deserving far more attention than that provided in this book is the issue of bilingual education. In several chapters, I define, describe, and illustrate bilingual education and the nature of these programs. However, I do not discuss in any detail the extensive research or the political battles surrounding this controversial issue. My aim is to focus discussion on curricular and programmatic matters, including the specific school-related factors conducive to language learning. Other researchers, such as David Ramirez, Steve Krashen, Ann Willig, and Jim Crawford, have reviewed the research on bilingual education; and Reynaldo Macías, Terry Wiley, and Rosalie Pedalino Porter, to name just have few, have covered the political arguments made on this issue.

I am indebted to many for their help in writing this book. I am grateful for the support of a Faculty-Grant-in-Aid provided by Arizona State University. I am also thankful for the invaluable feedback on the initial book proposal and drafts of selected chapters from Celia Genishi, Jim Cummins, Jim Crawford, Steve Krashen, and on later drafts, Kerri Flanagan. I appreciate the support of my family, who, and in many ways, inspired the writing of this book. Finally, I thank Jeff McQuillan for his valuable feedback and advice and for his unwavering encouragement and support, without which this book would still be under construction.

CHAPTER 1

"Why Don't They Learn English?": Language Policy and Public Perception

Editorials are written about it, politicians ride to office on it, school and governmental policies are passed based upon it. It is perhaps one of the most prevalent beliefs in American education today: Immigrants resist learning English. What's more, it is said that immigrants cling to their home or heritage language, segregating themselves linguistically from mainstream society. Where do these assumptions originate? How do they affect national language policy? In what way do they influence school practices? The answers to these questions provide an important glimpse into the state of collective U.S. thinking toward language diversity that has far-reaching implications for the education of all children in this nation.

The belief that immigrants resist learning English is so widespread that legislation has been authored to encourage immigrants and their children to learn and to speak it. The first of the most recent series of proposed constitutional amendments was introduced in 1981 to establish English as the official language of the United States. The amendment, presented by Senator S. I. Hayakawa of Hawaii, was designed to virtually outlaw the conduct of governmental business, including the offering of social services, in languages other than English. Hayakawa's amendment failed to pass Congress, but it was effective in reinvigorating a debate on language restrictionism, which continues at the national level to this day, with the reintroduction of similar amendments every few years. Individual states have also taken up the movement and have had more success. As of 2000, 20 states have official English laws and over a dozen other states have comparable types of legislation pending.[1]

In addition to English-only legislation, recent state propositions have cropped up to address a related belief: Not only do immigrants resist learning English, their children are failing to learn the language. In California, for example, the ballot initiative Proposition 227, dubbed the "Unz initiative" after its principal sponsor, "requires that all instruction be given in English," limiting teachers from using other languages for instruction.[2] This anti–bilingual education initiative passed in 1998 is expressly predicated on the notion that students are not learning English well. As I discuss in the following chapter, information available from federal government surveys and other sources call these conclusions into question and paint a different picture of the linguistic situation in immigrant communities.[3]

OFFICIAL ENGLISH-LANGUAGE AMENDMENTS

The pervasiveness of this resistance-to-English notion is evident in many public arenas, including in the United States Congress. As I mentioned earlier, in the past 20 years, more than half a dozen English-language amendments have been debated on the congressional floor. Carl Grove, as part of his doctoral dissertation research, compiled speeches given on English-language amendments from 1981 to 1998. A closer look at these policy makers' speeches reveals a core set of reasons consistently used to argue in favor of the amendments, many of them grounded in the notion that English is not being learned by new arrivals.

In Table 1.1, I have compiled a list of the rationale used by members of Congress in proposing official English-language constitutional amendments during the 17-year period between 1981 and 1998. Only speeches made when proposing or reintroducing the amendments were included in this analysis, excluding speeches made later in support of such amendments by other policy makers.

In the 15 speeches given over this period, the most commonly used argument—mentioned in 13 speeches—is that the English language itself is the glue that holds our society together and this cohesiveness is currently being threatened by multilingualism. Remarks such as those by Senator Huddleston of Kentucky, who reintroduced an official English-language amendment to the Constitution in 1983, illustrate these views:

> There are many nations in the world today that would give a great deal to have the kind of internal social and political stability that a single primary language (English) has afforded us. For us to consciously make the decision to throw away this stabilizing force would be seen as foolish and stupid in countries that have paid a high price for not having a universally accepted language.[4]

Citing bilingual nations with political instability, Huddleston claimed:

> Bilingualism . . . has torn apart communities from Canada to Brittany, from Belgium to India. It expresses not a sense of tolerance but a demand for di-

TABLE 1.1. Frequency of Reasons Given in Congressional Speeches for Supporting English-Language Amendments, 1981–1998

Rationale Given for Supporting English-Language Amendments	Number of Speeches Containing Rationale
English unites the country/Multilingualism is divisive	13
Once immigrants are in America, they should learn English/English needs to be preserved as the national language	10
Immigrants need motivation/It's for their own good	10
Foreign language programs and private use of other languages not affected	10
Immigrants are not learning English/Bilingual education is preventing English learning	7
Immigrants are not assimilating	3
Providing services in non-English languages is costly	2
Previous generations didn't need special language accommodations	1
Other countries have official languages and so should the United States	1

visions. . . . In countless places, differences in language have either caused or contributed significantly to political, social and economic instability. While the absence of language differences does not guarantee that these problems will not occur, I believe that it does significantly reduce the chances that they will occur.

Not only is the unity of U.S. society being threatened, according to proponents, so too is English as the national language. Ten of the speeches warned that if English is not actively preserved as the national language, then another language—such as Spanish—is likely to take its place. Senator Shumway noted the precarious position of English in his 1989 speech to propose yet another English-language amendment:

> The purpose of the amendment is simple: To provide our common language with the measure of legal protection which it now enjoys as a result of custom only. English is the common glue which has forged unity and strength from our rich cultural diversity. In my view, it is the primary language in which our government should continue to function. However, without that missing measure of legal protection, I believe that the primacy of English is being threatened.[5]

A related argument found in these speeches is that recent immigrants, unlike those of previous generations, are not motivated to learn English, due to the availability of services in other languages, such as bilingual ballots and bilingual education, a sentiment mentioned in seven speeches. Senator Symms called bilingual ballots and bilingual education "divisive measures,"[6] and Senator Symms contended that "[w]e have removed the heat from the 'melting pot,' and the melting seems to have very nearly stopped. Many Americans now feel like strangers in their own neighborhoods, aliens in their own country."[7]

Many argued, in fact, that it is for the immigrants' own good that a national language be established so that there will no longer be any excuses for not learning the language.[8] The government will thus cease to send out mixed messages that the lack of English fluency is acceptable, a point made in 10 speeches. Senator Shelby explained this logic:

> The inability to communicate fosters frustration and resentment. By encouraging people to communicate in a common language, we actually help them progress in society. A common language allows individuals to take advantage of the social and economic opportunities America has to offer. The ability to maintain a law abiding citizenry is hindered and the ability to offer true representation is certainly hampered if individuals cannot communicate their opinions.[9]

The alternative, Shelby warned, is linguistic segregation: "Efforts to create pockets of other language usage result in language enclaves and discrimination. Individuals living within the realm of particular subcultures are left out of the common fold."[10]

Members of Congress were quick to point out, however, that they were not against the use of languages other than English *if* English is the native tongue. Foreign-language programs will not be affected, and neither will the use of other languages for religious and cultural purposes, stated in 10 speeches.

It would seem that for native English speakers these arguments do not apply. The central issue, then, is that immigrants are not learning English, they must learn English, and when they do, they will have the same privilege of knowing another language. At that time, multilingualism will no longer pose a threat to national unity because the common language of English will be spoken by all. According to these arguments, if it can be shown that immigrants and their children *are* learning English to a high degree, then the rationale for restricting non-English languages would be moot.

EDUCATION SANCTIONS

Official English is one type of language policy based on the notion that immigrants don't learn English. Another involves how students are educated. The belief that immigrant children are not learning English properly or sufficiently quickly has resulted in restrictions placed on whether non-English languages can be used in schools, and by educators in their instruction. An indication of public sentiment on this issue can be found on the opinion pages of newspapers and news magazines. A colleague and I conducted a study on persuasive writing—editorials and letters to the editor—on bilingual education over a 10-year period, between 1984 and 1994.[11] We looked at 87 editorials and letters to the editor in five national newspapers and three national news magazines: *Los Angeles Times, New York Times, Christian Science Monitor, Washington Post, Wall Street Journal, Time, Newsweek,* and *U.S. News and World Report.* When we looked at the arguments made against bilingual education in these publications, we found many of the same reasons used to support English-only amendments in Congress (see Table 1.2).

Of the editorials and letters to the editor we examined, 20% argued that bilingual education segregates students, thereby slowing their integration into American society. Using a similar rationale presented in Congress, Richard D. Lamm wrote in a 1986 *New York Times* editorial:

> The United States is at a crossroads. If it does not consciously move toward greater integration, it will inevitably drift toward more fragmentation. It will either have to do better in assimilating all of the other peoples in its boundaries or it will witness increasing alienation and fragmentation. Cultural divisiveness is not a bedrock upon which a nation can be built. It is inherently unstable.[12]

Harold Evans, editorial director of *U.S. News and World Report*, also warned in 1986 that "[b]ilingualism has become a badge of separateness, not a route to assimilation."[13]

TABLE 1.2. Reason Given for Opposing Bilingual Education in Opinion Writing (N = 87)
(Excerpted from McQuillan & Tse, 1996)

	Percentage of Articles Citing Rationale
Effective/not effective in helping students learn English and achieve academically	51%
Leads to segregation of students/hampers assimilation	20%
Leads to anti-Americanism and divisive	19%

Another recurring theme that emerges from anti–bilingual education opinion articles is that bilingualism is itself divisive and anti-American. Nineteen percent of the articles argued that bilingual education contributes to the splintering of U.S. society. A staff editorial published in the *New York Times* in 1985, for example, stated: "English is the pot in which the melting takes place. Failure to speak and understand the American language hampers any citizen's ability to participate in American life."[14] George Will echoed these sentiments in a 1985 *Newsweek* editorial:

> Bilingualism, by suggesting that there is no duty to acquire the primary instrument of public discourse, further dilutes the idea of citizenship . . . [i]t is wrong to make a romance of linguistic diversity. Americans should say diverse things, but in a language that allows universal participation in the discussion.[15]

Jonathan Yardley, a columnist for the *Washington Post*, made the case in a 1994 editorial that the Bilingual Education Act of 1968 had been carried too far. In fact, "[s]oon 'bilingualism' became not a means of easing people into an English-speaking culture but, as special-interest groups found voice, one of perpetuating and reinforcing native cultures at the expense of English and, thus, Americanization."[16]

But the most often cited reason for opposing bilingual education—mentioned in more than 50% of the articles—is the idea that bilingual education is not effective in teaching students English. Luis Acle, Jr., claimed in a *Los Angeles Times* editorial, for example: "In the U.S., a student may graduate from high school without learning how to speak, read, and write in English," because students are permitted to take subject-matter exams in their native language until they reach grade-level proficiency.[17] Rosalie Pedalino Porter, a retired teacher and the author of the 1990 anti–bilingual education book *Forked Tongue*, maintained in an editorial:

> For two decades, federal- and state-funded bilingual education programs throughout the country have failed to prepare language-minority children for high school graduation, much less for jobs or higher education. Moreover, they have conspicuously failed to reduce the extraordinarily high drop-out rate for Latino students.[18]

Other editorials cited as evidence anecdotes and unpublished school-district reports that purportedly show bilingual education's failure in teaching students English. But these seem to confirm the author's already held opinions about how limited-English students were performing, as evidenced by the comment that "[s]urely no one will be particularly surprised to learn that the results [of New York's bilingual education program] thus far are negative."[19]

These same arguments continue to be used in more recent bilingual education debates.[20] In 1998, California voters passed Proposition 227, which eliminated bilingual education programs and put in their place a one-year intensive English-only program. Its proponents, including its chief backer, Ron Unz, claimed that nearly all children in bilingual education programs failed to learn English. In a 1997 editorial in the *Los Angeles Times*, Unz wrote:

> As one might expect, the results of such an approach to English instruction [bilingual education] are utterly dismal. Of the 1.3 million California schoolchildren—a quarter of our state's total public school enrollment—who begin each year classified as not knowing English, only about 5% learn English by year's end, implying an annual failure rate of 95% for existing programs.[21]

Others also complain of the dismal state of English learning among students, again pointing to bilingual education as the culprit. A letter to the editor by Art Pedroza, Jr., in the *Orange County Register*, stated,

> Indeed those trying to reform California's failed bilingual education program can point to statistics that show that a high percentage of children who are not immediately immersed in English and are instead ensnared in bilingual education do not go on to finish high school or enroll in college.[22]

In addition, nativism continues to appear on the opinion pages. Brenda Smith of San Diego believes that immigrants are getting preferential treatment among minorities: "As an African-American woman who has seen the assault on affirmative action, it galls me that immigrants can just walk into this country and demand and be given my tax dollars for their children from day one."[23]

Public opinion on how well children are learning English, as indicated by newspaper opinion pages, mirrors policy-maker views that immigrants and their children are not learning English quickly enough or well enough, and the use of languages other than English in school is to blame. These two indicators of public opinion—congressional speeches and press opinion articles—show quite clearly, I think, that this belief is widespread among Americans and is at the root of many attempts to pass language-restrictionist policy.

Are English-language learners in fact resisting English? Are they unaware of the need to learn English? Are they and their children failing to learn the new language? To address these questions, in the following chapter I will examine how well children and adults are learning English in linguistically diverse communities in the United States.

CHAPTER 2

The State of English-Language Learning

"Why don't they learn English?" is a question I have heard asked many times in one form or another. Sometimes the question is posed with genuine interest and concern, and other times, asked rhetorically in exasperation or with surprising vehemence. Whatever the driving sentiment, this question is predicated on the assumption that immigrants and their children don't want to learn English and resist doing so.

This belief may stem from the apparent ready and pervasive access to non-English languages in many communities in the United States. When we turn on the television we see Spanish-language programs, walking down the street we see billboards in non-English languages, and driving through many large cities we encounter store signs and services available in other languages. Faced with this apparent easy access to immigrant languages, one might conclude that immigrants are not learning English and are instead relying solely on their native language.

In Chapter 1, I showed the prevalence of this belief among policy makers and the general public. Politicians and the media bemoan today's unmotivated immigrants who, unlike their predecessors from decades ago, are not recognizing the need to learn the new language. For that reason, they argue, legislation is needed to compel immigrants to learn English and to do so quickly. Without such intervention, dire consequences would result, such as the expansion of immigrant pockets beyond their current enclave communities, which would lead to English no longer being the dominant language of the land and to ultimately dividing the nation across linguistic lines.

In this chapter, I look at these assumptions about the state of English-language learning among immigrants and their children to gauge whether there is any basis for concerns over the lack of immigrant assimilation. To set the stage, I begin by providing some figures on immigration past and present in the United States and then present information from a number of research studies, including several national and large-scale investigations on English-language learning among immigrant adults and their children. I conclude the chapter by discussing some of the obstacles to English-language learning in the United States and their impact on English language attainment.

WHO ARE U.S. IMMIGRANTS?

One stark difference between immigration at the turn of the 20th century and on the eve of the 21st is the countries from which immigrants are coming. Whereas most newcomers to the United States in 1900 were from Europe, in 1990 the majority of immigrants were from Latin America and Asia. As we can see in Figure 2.1, in 1900, Asia and Latin American entries constituted a mere 2%, while in 1990, these two sending regions totaled nearly three quarters of the foreign-born population, representing a dramatic cultural and linguistic shift.

FIGURE 2.1. Percent Foreign Born by Region of Birth, 1900 and 1990 (Adapted from Lapham, 1993)

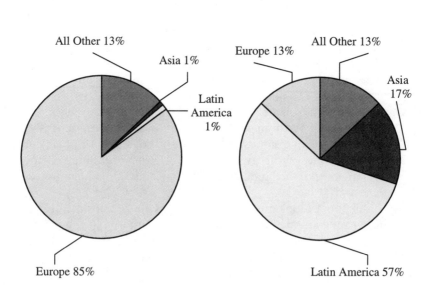

As of July 1999, those who were 5 years old and older and born outside the United States made up more than 10% of the U.S. population.[1] As Table 2.1 shows, the largest group of arrivals are from Mexico, making up 27.2%; followed in a distant second by immigrants from the Philippines, at 4.4%; then China and Hong Kong, at 4.3%; and Cuba at 3.5%. The other sending countries include Vietnam (3%), India (2.9%), the Dominican Republic (2.5%), El Salvador (2.4%), Great Britain (2.4%), and Korea (2.3%).

So, just how many immigrants are there in the United States? As of December 1999, approximately 25.8 million reside in the United States. If we look at the raw figures, the number of those foreign born in 1999 is the highest ever in U.S. history, as we can see in Figure 2.2. However, a better way to judge the impact of non-U.S.-born populations is to look at the *proportion* of the overall population made up of those born elsewhere. Contrary to popular belief, that percentage has gone down since the beginning of the 1900s. As Figure 2.3 shows, people born outside the United States in 1900 made up 13.6% of the population, while in 1999, the proportion is just 10.6%, down a significant 28%.

TABLE 2.1. Number and Percentage of U.S. Foreign Born and Country of Origin (From Lapham, 1993)

Country of Origin	Foreign-born March 1997 Number (percentage)
All countries	25,779,000 (100.0%)
Mexico	7,017,000 (27.2%)
Philippines	1,132,000 (4.4%)
China & Hong Kong	1,107,000 (4.3%)
Cuba	913,000 (3.5%)
Vietnam	770,000 (3.0%)
India	748,000 (2.9%)
Dominican Republic	632,000 (2.5%)
El Salvador	607,000 (2.4%)
Great Britain	606,000 (2.4%)
Korea	591,000 (2.3%)

FIGURE 2.2. Foreign-Born Population, 1900–1999 (in millions) (Data for 1900 to 1990: Lapham, 1993. Data for 1999: U.S. Bureau of the Census, 2000. Retrieved April 2, 2000 from the World Wide Web: http://www.census.gov/population/estimates/nation/nativity/fbtab002.txt)

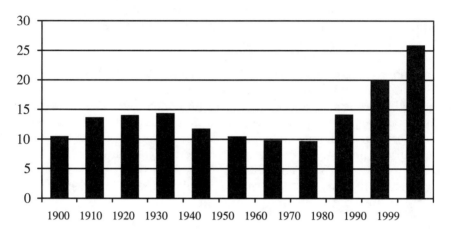

Even though there are proportionally fewer immigrants now than 90 years ago, English-language learning remains an important issue among the foreign-born population. In fact, during the 1990s, the number of children who are limited-English speakers has steadily increased, as we can see in Figure 2.4, primarily due to immigration. In the 1990–91 school year, about 2.2 million students in U.S. schools had limited proficiency in English. That figure steadily rose to reach approximately 3.5 million in 1996–97, a remarkable increase of nearly 60% over that 6-year period.

What do these and other population figures tell us about the current state of English-language learning? First, there were proportionally more immigrants in the United States at the turn of the 20th century than at the turn of the 21st, and yet English in the early 1900s did not cease to be the sole dominant language and the language of prestige of the nation. Second, we need to keep in mind that immigrants today have even more compelling reasons to learn English and they seem to be well aware of these advantages (see Chapter 3 for a further discussion). While it was possible for those living, for instance, in 1910 to make a living in farming or in a trade without a high school diploma and high levels of English literacy, today's service-oriented economy makes it difficult to earn a living without these qualifications (see Chapter 4).

FIGURE 2.3. Percentage of Foreign Born of U.S Population (1900–1990 figures from Rong & Preissle, 1998; 1999 percentage computed by taking the 1999 general U.S. population figure and the number of foreign-born from Figure 2.2)

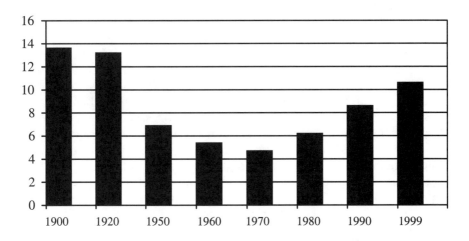

FIGURE 2.4. English Language Learner Enrollment Growth, 1990–91 to 1996–97 (Macías, 1998. Retrieved February 12, 2000 from the World Wide Web: http://www.ncbe.gwu.edu/ncbepubs/seareports/96-97/f3.htm)

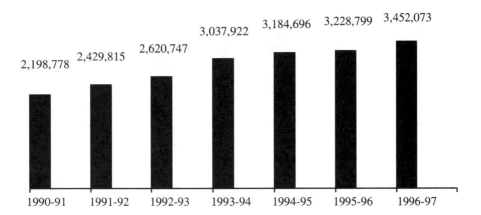

ARE IMMIGRANTS AND THEIR CHILDREN LEARNING ENGLISH?

Despite a growing influx of immigrants to the United States from non-English-speaking countries, the large majority of immigrants *are learning English and learning it well*. U.S. Census data shows that among foreign-born residents, nearly *three quarters* of those 5 years of age or older spoke English "well" or "very well" in both 1979 and 1989, as Table 2.2 shows. This is rather extraordinary considering that the number of new immigrants to the United States increased by almost 75% in this 10-year period. Given that nearly all immigrants speak a language other than English, the fact that the percentage of adults reporting a good command of English held steady shows that immigrants are doing remarkably well.

These signs that immigrants are learning English hold true even for states with large numbers of immigrants. Florida, for instance, has the third largest population of Spanish-speaking residents, with about 1.6 million. Researcher Thomas D. Boswell of the University of Miami looked at 1990 U.S. Census data to see whether immigrants are learning English in that state and to examine the economic impact of non-English languages in the region.[2] He found that immigrants and their children are indeed learning to speak English. Among the Spanish-speaking immigrants arriving in the United States before 1950, 81% reported being able to speak English well or very well, and those who arrived later—between 1982 and

TABLE 2.2. English Language Ability of Persons 5 and Over by Language Spoken at Home and Number of Foreign-Born Entries, 1979 and 1989 (Adapted from MacArthur, 1993. Also see Krashen & McQuillan, 1995, and U.S. Bureau of Census, 1997)

	1979		1989	
	Foreign Born: 4,935,000*		Foreign Born: 8,555,000*	
	Spanish	Asian/Pacific Islander	Spanish	Asian/Pacific Islander
well/very well	71.8	73.8	71.5	72.3
not well/not at all	28.2	26.2	28.5	27.7

*figures for 1970–1979 and 1980–1989, respectively.

1990—more than 50% claimed no difficulty speaking the language. This last figure is particularly impressive when we consider that when the 1990 Census was taken, some of those included in the analysis may have been in the United States for as little as 1 to 3 years. This evidence is a good sign of rapid progress toward learning English, with immigrants continuing to improve their ability over time, speaking the language better the longer they are in the United States. The children of immigrants born in the United States are also learning English. In Boswell's analysis of Florida residents, more than 94% of immigrant children spoke English well or very well.

Even among immigrant groups thought to live in isolated "language ghettos," English-language learning is taking place at high levels. A recent survey of immigrants from four Spanish-speaking populations living in the United States—Colombians, Dominicans, Guatemalans, and Salvadorans—found that a large majority report understanding English well or very well (see Figure 2.5).[3] The participants in the study reported high levels of English comprehension, despite the fact that the majority were fairly recent immigrants and arrived as adults in the United States. More than 75% from Colombia said they understood English well or very well, followed closely by the Salvadorans at 73.3%, Guatemalans at 66.6%, and Dominicans at 62.9%. Far fewer reported having difficulty with English, understanding it not well or not at all: Colombian (24.7%), Salvadorans (26.6%), Guatemalans (33.3%), and Dominicans (37.1%).[4]

The figures on adult English proficiency are very encouraging. They show that a large majority of those born outside of the United States are learning the language well. That's not to say that immigrants have no dif-

FIGURE 2.5. Percentage Speaking "Well" or "Very Well" Among Four Spanish-speaking Populations in the U.S. (Adapted from National Association of Latino Elected and Appointed Officials Education Fund and The Tomás Rivera Policy Institute Report, 1998)

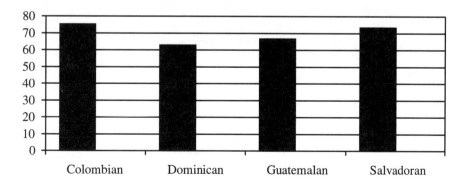

ficulty with the language, but the data available indicates that for fairly large segments of the foreign-born population, rather than becoming stagnant in their English ability, the longer immigrants live in the U.S., the more likely they are to be proficient in the language. On the basis of this information, there are no signs that adult immigrants shy away from learning English. In fact, they seem to be doing remarkably well.

Lisa is one of these successful immigrants. Originally from Hong Kong, Lisa moved to the United States with her parents and three siblings when she was 20 years old. Two years earlier, she had spent a year living with her aunt in Canada and studying English as a foreign language at the age of 18. When her family immigrated to Arizona, her parents opened a small gift shop, and Lisa worked at the store part of the day, spending the balance of her time working at her uncle's restaurant. She recalled that at this time, she had a lot of difficulty with English. Each time she wanted to say something in the language, she would have to carefully consider how to put her thoughts into the new language, often translating from her native Chinese. She recalled many instances when people had trouble understanding her choppy and heavily accented English.

Fortunately for Lisa, she had completed high school and a few basic junior college accounting courses before coming to the United States. These qualifications helped her land a job as a bookkeeper at a local bank 6 months after her arrival. Luckily, this position required fluency with numbers, not English. Lisa, who is personable and outgoing, starting making friends with her English-speaking co-workers, and after 2½ years, she spoke the language well enough to be promoted to bank teller, which required her to speak English and to interact with English native speakers on a daily basis in her almost exclusively English-speaking community. Lisa eventually took a job working for the U.S. Postal Service, where she moved up the ranks for nearly 18 years, making a good living to support herself, and eventually her son, as a single mom. In 1999, she quit her postal job to open her own business as a party planner. For nearly 20 years, Lisa has been an avid reader of mystery and suspense novels, is now a regular user of the Internet, and takes care of all matters personal and professional in English. While she still has a noticeable accent and makes occasional grammatical errors in writing, she is a proficient and confident user of the language.[5]

Her success is not emblematic of all immigrant cases, however, and illustrates how background circumstances may influence how well new arrivals fare in the United States. Those who are educated in the home country and have the resources and opportunity to study the language formally, for instance, are at a distinct advantage over those who immigrate with little money or formal schooling. Imagine if Lisa had not graduated from high school or taken college courses in Hong Kong, and did not have the financial resources to study English abroad for a year. It is unlikely that she would have been offered a job at a bank, a job that gave her financial independence as well as regular and social contact with fluent English speakers, leading eventually to better jobs and more social integration. Without those qualifications, she would still perhaps be working part-time as a store clerk or waitress, which could have had an important impact on how well she learned English and whether she would ever have reached financial self-sufficiency. These background factors explain, in large part, why some immigrant families make it into the American mainstream while others linger on the social and economic margins.

English-Language Acquisition among Children of Immigrants

The studies mentioned so far give an overall picture of English-language learning in the United States. Considering the concern in public debates and the media over how children of immigrants are learning English and achieving in schools, let's take a closer look at how well children who immigrated with their parents and those born in the United States are faring.

Despite reports to the contrary, immigrant children have been very successful if we look at two important indicators: students' general level of English proficiency and their school achievement. Research studies bearing on these keys to success lead to the same conclusion: Immigrant children are acquiring English well and with striking rapidity, and they are doing well in U.S. schools given the linguistic barriers they face.

One of the most recent and thorough examinations of how well children learn English in the United States is a large-scale project conducted by two sociologists, Alejandro Portes of Princeton University and his colleague, Lingxin Hao of Johns Hopkins. These researchers surveyed more than 5,000 eighth- and ninth-grade students in two of the country's largest immigrant communities, Miami–Fort Lauderdale, Florida; and San Diego, California. Both inner-city and suburban schools were included in their study, with students from a number of different national origins, including those of Latin American, Asian, and Caribbean heritage. The researchers focused specifically on the children of immigrants.[6]

Their results in terms of both English-language proficiency and language preferences show just how well immigrant children are learning English, as Figure 2.6 shows.

All immigrant groups, regardless of educational background or social class, had overall high levels of self-reported English proficiency. Researchers have found that self-reported language levels, including English ability

FIGURE 2.6. Percent of Students Reporting Speaking English "Well" or "Very Well" (Adapted from Portes & Hao, 1998)

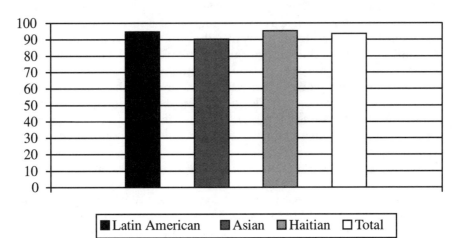

reported in surveys studies such as the U.S. census, are strongly correlated with actual test scores of language proficiency.[7] Nearly all students in the study—an overwhelming 93.6%—noted being able to speak English "well" or "very well," and the figures were similar across the three groups: Haitian (95.4%), Latin American (94.7%), and Asian (90.3%). Even more interesting is the data the researchers gathered on these same students' language preferences. Almost three fourths of the students said they not only knew English well, they preferred to speak it over their native tongue.

An even more impressive study showing the strength of English-language learning among immigrant children is found in Xue Lue Rong and Judith Preissle's analysis of data from the 1990 U.S. Census.[8] These researchers looked at data *only* on children who were born outside of the United States, a group much less likely to report speaking English well than the mostly U.S.-born students in Portes and Hao's study discussed earlier. Yet Rong and Preissle found that even among children who had been born outside of the United States, the level of self-reported English language proficiency was very high. Of the more than 2.2 million foreign-born children age 5 to 18, 86.8% reported speaking English "well" or "very well." This is made even more remarkable by the fact that more than *half* of these children had been in the United States for less than 5 years, and one third for less than 3 years. In short, immigrant children are acquiring English at an astoundingly rapid pace.

Perhaps the most telling sign of the dominance of English in the lives of immigrant children is the defining role that the language plays in their school and social lives. Take, for example, the students at Nimitz Middle School in Huntington Park, California. In 1995, Nimitz enrolled more than 3,000 students, 97% of whom were Latino. If you visit the lunchroom, the playground, or the hallways, you will see two distinct groups: those who are born in the United States and speak fluent English and those recent immigrants still learning the language. In this school as in many others, how well you speak English determines in large part your status in the school, with the new immigrants at the bottom of that ladder. Gabriela Rico, an eighth-grader at the school, tells of how she is teased and mocked by the English-fluent U.S.-born students in gym class because she doesn't understand the games they play. And yet, she says that what she and the other immigrant students want most is "to learn the games, to learn English, to be like them."[9] Among these students and other immigrant students across the country, English fluency is a badge of prestige, a membership card for entry into the mainstream. English is one of the primary keys to fitting in and being accepted.

Academic Performance among Children of Immigrants

The exceptionally high rate of English-language acquisition among immigrant youth is matched in many ways by their academic performance. While many immigrant students struggle with language and cultural differences in schools, most have been quite successful given the barriers to success they face. Alejandro Portes and another sociologist, Ruben Rumbaut of Michigan State University, examined the academic performance of immigrant students in San Diego area high schools for 3 years, 1986, 1989, and 1992. As was the case with Portes's study on English-language acquisition mentioned earlier, their results were counter to public perceptions about the level of school success among immigrants in the United States. Gathering data from a group of more than 12,000 sophomores, juniors, and seniors, these researchers compared the grade point averages (GPA) of students who spoke only English ("English-only"), those who spoke fluent English and another language ("Fluent English Proficient"), and those who were still limited in English proficiency ("Limited English Proficient"). Figure 2.7 shows this GPA comparison of all three groups.

What stands out from Portes and Rumbaut's study is how well immigrant students perform compared to their native-English-speaking counterparts. The Limited English Proficient (LEP) students who are still learning English have nearly the same GPA as those who are English fluent (2.06

FIGURE 2.7. Academic Performance (GPA) of Immigrant High School Students in San Diego by Language Status, 1989 (Adapted from Portes & Rumbaut, 1996)

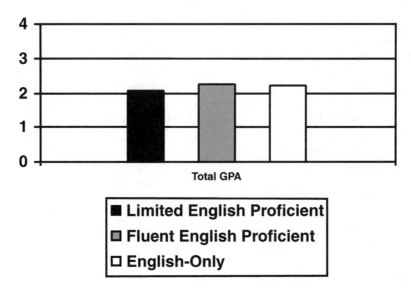

versus 2.23)! This is a stunning outcome, considering that LEP students are still at a considerable language disadvantage compared to the largely native-born English-only students. We should expect students still learning English to do considerably worse than their English-only peers. Those who were classified Fluent English Proficient (FEP), students who speak English and another language, actually received slightly *higher* grades than English-fluent students (2.27). Data collected from two other groups of students from San Diego, one in 1986 and another in 1992, confirmed these results, with LEP trailing English-only students by only a small margin, and FEP students outperforming both groups.[10] Judging from these outcomes, immigrant students are clearly doing well in school, considering the language challenges they start out with. In fact, those who grow up in homes where a language other than English is spoken actually outperform monolingual English speakers once they themselves are fluent in English.

Portes and Rumbaut also examined drop-out rates among the three groups of students. Once again, immigrant students perform much better than expected. Not surprisingly, those students who were still classified as LEP had higher drop-out rates than English-only students, 14.4% versus

7.8%. Yet immigrant students fluent in English had a nearly identical drop-out rate to English-only students, 7.7%. Once immigrant students over-come the linguistic hurdle of learning English, they are as likely as English-only students to stay in school.

Further evidence on the performance of immigrant children in school comes from Rong and Preissle's study mentioned earlier, which analyzed 1990 Census data. In addition to examining English-language proficiency, these researchers also studied the educational attainment of immigrants. They found that, similar to Portes and Rumbaut's conclusions, immigrant students nationally were often doing as well as native-born, native-English-speaking students. Students who were still limited in English had, as might be expected, higher drop-out rates than native-English speakers, whether they came from families of high or low income. But foreign-born students who were now fluent in English had the same or lower drop-out rates than English-only students.[11]

In fact, a more sophisticated analysis of drop-out data among more than 1,700 Hispanic/Latino students, conducted by Anne Driscoll, showed that immigrant students actually did as well as and sometimes better than U.S.-born students of U.S.-born parents, that is, third-generation children.[12] Driscoll examined the effects of various influences on school drop-out, including which generation the students were born into, parent's income and education, and student GPA. Taking these important factors into ac-count, Driscoll found that the overall drop-out rate for first generation Hispanic/Latino immigrant students was no greater than for those who were third generation, that is, the children of U.S.-born parents. She also found that second-generation students—those born in the United States with at least one foreign-born parent—were *half* as likely to drop out than third-generation students. What this tells us is that when important and relevant factors are taken into account, immigrant students do as well as or better than other students in terms of academic progress through high school.[13] Although there is some variation in performance across ethnic groups and the originating country, immigrant children perform remark-ably well overall both in terms of English-language proficiency and in academic achievement and progress.[14]

WHY DO SOME STUDENTS LEARN
ENGLISH FASTER THAN OTHERS?

A controversy related to the question of whether immigrants and their children are learning English is how fast they are learning the language. The evidence presented in this chapter shows that students are learning

English with remarkable speed, contrary to the public's perception, but that's not to say that all students learn the language at the same rate. The rate at which immigrants acquire English is not solely dependent upon how long a person has resided in the United States. Studies show that factors related to income and education also affect how quickly immigrants will acquire English, as we saw in the case of Lisa, who immigrated from Hong Kong at the age of 20. This is true for both children and adults. Among children, in the analysis by Rong and Preissle mentioned earlier, the researchers found that those who come from high-income families tend to report higher levels of English than those from low-income families.

Family income and educational background are important in determining language learning success, but it is not these factors *per se* that influence life outcomes, but rather, the benefits they afford. For instance, students from wealthier homes are more likely to have received schooling in the native language back in their home country. More schooling in the native language helps immigrant students build more background knowledge in academic subjects so that when they arrive in the United States, they are better equipped to understand the tasks they encounter in school and pick up English faster as a result. Students from high-income homes may also have more educational resources at home, such as books and reference materials. More access to educational resources makes it easier for children to develop better literacy skills that aid them in both academic performance and language acquisition in a school environment. Better reading and writing allows them, for example, to more easily understand the concept of writing stories and to navigate a textbook. Finally, students from upper-income families may have more opportunities to interact with English speakers outside of enclave communities. Those who are of higher income tend to have more connections with the English-speaking world outside of their own cultural community. Each of these advantages has a direct impact on English-language learning. Similar findings have been reported for adult immigrants. Adults who have received more formal education in their native language acquire English more rapidly than those with less formal education, taking into account their length of residence in an English-speaking country.[15]

Stephen Krashen, a researcher at the University of Southern California, addressed in a recent book the frequent claim that students from Asia tend to be more successful than Latino students. He rightly points out that the critical factor is not the cultural heritage of the students;[16] instead, the quality of the child's education in the first language, although not the only determinant, makes a critical difference for academic success. Children who enter U.S. schools having been formally educated in the home country may have two important benefits—background knowledge in school subjects and literacy in the native language—which contribute to educational success in U.S. schools (I elaborate on these factors in chapters 4 and 5). For instance, Southeast Asian students from Cambodia and Laos who have had little or no formal education are likely to face some of the same formidable challenges as are the Salvadoran and Guatemalan students who arrive from rural areas with little experience in academic settings such as those found in the United States. At the same time, a child from the relatively wealthy community of Monterey, Mexico, who has attended a private, college-prep high school may have some of the same advantages as a student from Korea who also attended the same type of school. The background experiences of each of these students will greatly influence their educational attainment in the United States, for better or worse.

Because building previous experiences that mirror those found in U.S. schools is one key to academic success, schools and communities may be able to provide students with some of these same advantages and help level the playing field. In a study I conducted in 1999, I examined the life histories of 10 college students who managed to become biliterate—able to read and write well in two languages—despite having been raised in the United States and having spent little time in the native country. More than half of the 10 students I interviewed came from working-class homes and had parents who did not complete high school. Despite this, all these students of Latino and Asian backgrounds were enrolled at a community college or 4-year university and reported being in good standing. All 10 were fluent and highly proficient in English. The key, in part, seems to have been the native language and literacy support they received in the community and in school.[17]

We also need to keep in mind that although standardized tests provide important information about student achievement, there are cognitive and linguistic abilities less susceptible to pencil-and-paper measures. What students are able to do in real-life situations gives us another indication of their skills. A good example of a skill that many immigrant students have but that is generally untapped by standardized tests is "language brokering," the interpretation and translation bilingual people conduct on behalf of others. A number of studies show that immigrant children often act as interpreters and translators for their parents and other people at home, in the community, and in school, and that conducting such tasks require sophisticated linguistic, cultural, and cognitive skill.[18]

Take the case of 14-year-old Ariela, the daughter of Mexican immigrants living in Chicago. On one Thursday afternoon, her mother receives a jury summons in the mail and Ariela reads it for her. Despite the technical language and Ariela's lack of familiarity with the concept of jury duty, she is able to communicate the contents to her mother. What's more, she is able to call the courthouse the following day with several questions raised by her mother and interpret between her mother and the official on the other end of the phone. She is also able to help her mother complete the reporting form as the notice directed.[19]

The tasks that "brokers" take on often require figuring out multiple sources of complex information intended for adults, so that important family decisions can be made. Two studies of bilingual high schoolers who speak Spanish, Vietnamese, Chinese, or a combination of these found that nearly all students surveyed had interpreted or translated for their families at one time or another. The few who had not performed these tasks themselves said that an older sibling in the family took on that responsibility.[20]

Anita is the oldest child in her family and the designated broker. Anita is trilingual, having been raised in Mexico and then having immigrated to the United States at the age of 12. One day, just a few months after she immigrated, she sat at the kitchen table with her father to translate for him their mortgage statement. As we listen in, we hear her using three languages: Cantonese, her father's native language; English, the language of the document; and Spanish, which both she and her father speak. In front of her is the mortgage document and two dictionaries: a bilingual English-Chinese edition and a standard English dictionary. When she comes across words she doesn't know, she consults one or both of the dictionaries, shows the definition to her father in Chinese, uses Spanish to clarify or confirm the meaning, and eventually comes to some understanding of the unfamiliar English words. She has to understand not only the words on the page, but at least to some extent, also the complex principles behind mortgages and related financing concepts.[21]

Children such as Anita are critical to their families making the transition to life in the United States. Although children are not necessarily faster language learners, they typically have more opportunities to pick up the language from school and from peers. Parents who are still learning the language may, for a time, need their children to bridge communication, with the need for brokering lessening or ceasing once parents are able to communicate in English on their own.

The ability of children such as Anita and Ariela to perform these tasks demonstrates an understanding of adult issues in multiple languages, skills not easily or likely to be measured by school assessments. In many ways, immigrant children are doing even better than the studies we discussed previously indicate, since they are performing school tasks well in addition to taking on what are often complex, sophisticated, and demanding out-of-school bilingual tasks.

OBSTACLES TO LEARNING ENGLISH

Learning English is a necessity, not a luxury, for immigrants. Arrivals in earlier periods in history could labor on farms, work in factories, and build railroads without speaking fluent English or possessing much literacy. Today's service-oriented economy requires English ability for all but the lowest paying jobs. This reality is not lost on new arrivals to the United States.

When we look at the situation of adult English learners, a clear picture emerges of highly motivated learners but few English-language-learning support services. Although there are no definitive figures on how many adults need English as a second language (ESL) services in the United States, in 1997, approximately 1.8 million adults enrolled in ESL programs that received funding through the U.S. Department of Education, constituting 46% of the overall national adult education enrollment.[22] Considering that in 1997, more than 23 million adults age 18 and over were born outside the United States, and more than 8 million had been in the United States 10 years or less, and 4 million five years or less, the 1.8 million enrolled in federally funded ESL programs is a small proportion of those still likely to be limited in English.[23]

This may be a result of some formidable obstacles for adult immigrants to get formal schooling in English. In a 1995 nationally representative survey, U.S. adults were asked about six types of adult education programs, including English as a second language. Among those who expressed an interest in taking adult education courses but who were not enrolled, the top barriers to participation were the lack of time (47%), the prohibitive cost (30%), the need for child care (7%), and the lack of adequate transportation (3%).[24] A closer look at the daily lives of some immigrants illustrates how these and other types of limitations might interfere with English-language learning.

Chou Chang is a Hmong immigrant from Laos, one of more than 80,000 Hmong refugees who have been resettled in the United States beginning in 1979.[25] The Hmong are a hill tribe originally from China, who have settled in Southeast Asian countries over the past 150 years. The United States hired many of the Hmong to fight against the communist movement in Laos in the 1970s, and when the communist forces successfully gained power in 1975, those working for the United States had to flee, eventually being resettled in a number of cities in the United States.

Chou Chang is one of the many Hmong refugees resettled in Philadelphia.[26] Unlike many of the other refugees in his community, however, he possesses an important asset for learning English. He is one of the few

Hmong literate in Lao and has managed to complete his high school equivalency diploma. As research tells us, having literacy in one language makes
it easier to learn literacy in another (see Chapter 3 for further discussion),
and his high school equivalency diploma signals his readiness, at least to
some degree, to continue his education. And, in fact, Chou is studying to
improve his English at the local community college. However, for himself
and his family, the pressures of dealing with bureaucratic institutions, as
well as with members of the Hmong community, make it difficult for him
to attend to his English-language studies.

One Tuesday, Chou received a letter from his resettlement caseworker
informing him that he needed to report to her office Friday morning with
four documents in hand, or his case file would be closed. It was necessary
that one of the four documents be stamped by an agency several miles
from his home and not easily accessible by public transportation; and for
the others, he was required to pick up various forms and signatures from
different places. That evening, Chou called his English teacher to tell her
he would be absent, spending the time normally reserved for homework
fixing his bicycle because he knew it would be impossible to complete the
tasks on foot before that Friday.[27]

Chou often received requests from recently arrived members of the
community to write letters for them or to complete government forms on
their behalf. Social workers would also contact Chou, as an English-
speaking representative of the community. On one occasion, a social
worker from a neighboring church asked Chou to translate a sign from
English to Hmong. Chou once again put aside his homework, to write and
rewrite the message until it was to his satisfaction. On another occasion
when the phone rang incessantly while his homework remained neglected,
he shouted in exasperation, "Too many calls! Too many questions! . . .
Everybody want something from me!"[28] It is not difficult to see how navigating social services and responding to community demands can interfere with English learning, in this case despite Chou's motivation and com-
mitment to learning the language and his advantages over his fellow
refugees in terms of English proficiency and educational background.

Chou is able to enroll in ESL courses at the community college; in
many parts of the country, however, there is a shortage of ESL offerings
through adult education programs. According to a report sponsored by
the Clearinghouse on Adult, Career, and Vocational Education, there is
an insufficient number of programs and not enough room in existing ones
to serve all prospective English students.[29] In most cities, there are waiting lists of from several months to several years for immigrants wishing
to enroll in ESL classes, and many rural communities lack ESL programs
altogether.

A line of more than 500 people began forming at sunrise in Bellevue, Washington. These early risers are not waiting to buy concert tickets or to reserve a spot along a parade route. This is registration day at Bellevue Community College, which offers a free ESL program. The large crowd is made up of aspiring students from Ethiopia, Mexico, Korea, and the Ukraine, among other countries, and these immigrants know that demand for ESL classes far outstrips availability. Their hope is to get on the rolls and not on a long waiting list. Maria Garcia is now an employee at the college and continues to take advanced ESL courses after having arrived from Mexico more than 20 years ago. She expressed the importance she attaches to English in this way: "If we don't speak English, how are we going to live in America?" Alice Ferrier, executive director of the Eastside Literacy Council, which also sponsors free adult ESL classes, noted that there is no need to advertise the program. Simply through word of mouth, the courses always fill. She commented, "I don't think we have a real sense of all of the unmet need" for free or low-cost courses.[30]

In addition to the lack of available programs and the other obstacles mentioned earlier, immigrants may face further important limitations to participation in ESL classes. A disproportionate number of immigrant households fall below the poverty line, and many adult immigrants work multiple jobs and long hours to make a living. Even those with advanced educational qualifications and professional work experience in their home countries find themselves in menial and low-paying jobs in the United States. These professionals' credentials are often not recognized in the United States and they may lack the technical and specialized English needed to work in their respective fields. Being economically poor and living from paycheck to paycheck limits the amount of time available to devote to formal language study, adding to other obstacles such as insufficient funds for tuition and child care.

While some find steady employment, a large number of immigrants are seasonal workers who migrate from one part of the country to another throughout the year. A 1991 estimate indicated that there are more than 1.6 million migrant farmworkers in the United States.[31] Workers from Mexico, Guatemala, Puerto Rico, El Salvador, and other countries follow crop routes over the course of each year. The "eastern stream," for instance, travels from Texas and Florida through the mid-Atlantic states and New England to Maine. Working a typical 10 to 12 hours doing stoop labor while moving from farm to farm, these workers find few opportunities to participate in any social or educational programs, including those to learn English. Resources to pay tuition are also limited when typical jobs offer no benefits and pay an average of $4.80 per hour or by bushel at 40 cents for each bushel harvested.[32] Many migrant farmworkers travel with their families. Their children, many of whom are U.S. born, may go through two to four school systems in any one year, if they attend school at all.

Roxana Machado is 10 years old, the eldest of six children, and her parents are U.S. citizens. Her family has moved four times in the past year. Despite this, she speaks fluent English, likes school, and wants to earn a high school diploma. It's difficult to say, though, whether she will reach her goal considering her migratory lifestyle and the general lack of appropriate support services. There are some success stories, however. Juan Vera, a 17-year-old high school senior and son of a tomato picker, attends a magnet school in Virginia, where he excels in science and is considering a career in biomedical research. Angela Tejeda, the daughter of apple pickers, was the first migrant student to graduate high school in southwestern Virginia and went on to earn a bachelor's degree. These successes are relatively rare, but that they exist at all is astonishing, considering the formidable challenges migrant students face.[33]

Yet another obstacle that immigrants and their children encounter is unrealistic language expectations expressed most often toward adult English learners. When I hear people say that immigrants are not learning English, my mind conjures up a comical scene of people gesturing in vain to one another, hopping up and down in frustration in an effort to communicate. I've discovered over the years, however, that when people say immigrants are not learning English they usually mean that they don't sound like native speakers.

I realized the impact of these unrealistic expectations while making my way through graduate school teaching adult community ESL classes. Among those classes was an accent-reduction course that purportedly trained English-language learners to speak more like native speakers. Nearly all the students who enrolled in the classes were good speakers of English who encountered few communication problems in the language, and as I discovered to my surprise, for the most part their nonstandard accents caused them few misunderstandings. Why, then, did these immigrants pay hundreds of dollars and spend several evenings a week and Saturdays in an accent-reduction course?

As I got to know some of these students, their reasons became more evident. Some spoke of the alienation they felt from their native-speaker co-workers, while others recounted stories of being the butt of jokes, being avoided, and being ignored because they sounded different.[34] While these negative experiences drove many of these students to enroll in English courses to improve their English, these same experiences had the predictable effect of lowering students' confidence and their willingness to speak the language. As language researchers will attest, the psychological block that low language self-esteem erects has a downward-spiral effect.

The more uncomfortable learners feel using a new language, the fewer interactions they are likely to have with people who speak that language, which in turn limits how much they learn. By contrast, the more tolerance new language learners encounter, the more willing they are to use the language, and ultimately, to reach high levels of proficiency. A more effective strategy for encouraging language learning, then, would be to show acceptance rather than "tough love" disapproval.

In this chapter, I have presented strong evidence that immigrants are indeed learning English. Despite public perception to the contrary, children of immigrants are by and large learning English rapidly and succeeding in school. Important to note is that these achievements are being made in spite of formidable economic and social obstacles, including a high level of poverty and inadequate publicly supported English-language programs.

It is clear, then, that the question asked in the title of this book, "Why don't they learn English?" is based on an unsupported assumption that immigrants are not learning the language and are resistant to becoming English proficient. The language restrictionism advocated by policy makers and members of the public is, in fact, unnecessary. On the contrary, the primary language "problem" among most immigrants is not a lack of English-language learning, but rather, as I will discuss in the following chapters, the rapid loss of the immigrant languages across communities.

CHAPTER 3

The State of Heritage Language Development

I've been in many language-related discussions with friends, family, and the occasional stranger, but I rarely hear comments such as "If we don't do something soon, native languages are going to die out," or "It's a shame that home languages don't get more attention in schools."

The flip side of the false perception over failure of immigrants to learn English is their retention of the home or "heritage" language. In fact, heritage languages vanish from immigrant families as children learn English and prefer it over the home language. The issue of heritage language disappearance in the United States continues to elude public consciousness and concern, although this language loss across generations is, in my opinion, one of the most fundamental erosions of a national resource in this country.[1] In this chapter, I will discuss how and why language loss occurs and the reasons why preference for English takes hold early in a child's development. I will also address why the situation appears quite the opposite to the public, many of whom believe minority languages are being perpetuated through "language ghettoes."

THE TYPICAL LIFE OF AN IMMIGRANT LANGUAGE

Immigrant languages have short lives in the United States. By the grand-children's generation, the family stops using the non-English language at home, resulting in the third generation becoming largely monolingual in English. The typical pattern of language loss looks something like this: An adult immigrant arrives in the United States and learns enough English to operate in daily life, while continuing to use her stronger tongue—the heritage language—at home. She raises her children to speak the heritage language, but as these children enter school and learn English, they switch to English when speaking with their siblings and friends. By the time they graduate from elementary school, these same children are better speakers of English than they are of the home language and prefer using English in nearly every realm. When they grow up and have children of their own, English is typically the only language spoken in their own home, and these grandchildren have little to no familiarity with the heritage language.

This pattern has been observed across language groups and documented in a number of research studies.[2] One such study, published in 1998 by sociologists Alejandro Portes and Lingxin Hao, looked at the language ability of second-generation students, the children of immigrants.[3] These eighth- and ninth-graders were from 42 Miami–Fort Lauderdale and San Diego schools with relatively large numbers of immigrants from fairly concentrated communities, a setting where students would have a good chance of developing high levels of the home language. The researchers found that the teenagers knew English well. In terms of the heritage language, however, language loss was clearly evident. Among the Spanish-speaking students, fewer than half were fluent bilinguals, and among those of Asian background, fewer than 10% were. In terms of their preferences, two thirds favored using English over their parents' language.

The push to learn English is so strong that language shift—switching from using primarily the heritage language to English—can often occur *within* a lifetime.[4] Take the case of Rick, who arrived in the United States at the age of 4.[5] As a child, he spoke only Cantonese in the home with parents, sisters, and relatives. When he entered school, he learned to speak conversational English quite quickly, and by the fourth grade, spoke primarily English with classmates and friends. English was everywhere in his life: He watched TV and movies, learned school subjects, and played with friends in that language. While he still spoke some Cantonese with his parents, he preferred to use English with his older sisters. By the time he entered junior high, Rick could speak to his parents in his heritage language about typical family and household topics, but had difficulty talking about matters outside of the home, including what he learned at school. He studied the food chain in science, but doesn't know how to tell his mother about it over dinner—in Cantonese. He would like to tell his father about his plans for the future, but doesn't know the right words—in Cantonese. By the time Rick graduates high school, he can "get by" in conversational Cantonese, but is far from fluent. What a difference 12 years makes: Rick has gone from being monolingual in Cantonese to being nearly monolingual in English. It's hard to imagine a more thorough linguistic transformation.

There are, of course, exceptions to this general pattern.[6] However, this "subtractive bilingualism," where the native language stops developing as English is learned, is widespread, and the economic impact is clear.[7] Business owners in the Miami area have complained about the lack of biliterates—bilinguals able to read and write in both languages—needed to conduct business in Latin American markets.[8] This absence of biliterates is not surprising considering that literacy is the first victim of language loss across generations. Even if the second generation retains the ability to speak the language to some degree, reading and writing seldom gets developed to any appreciable level.

CAUSES OF LANGUAGE LOSS

The Powerful Pull of English

There are several reasons why heritage languages fight an uphill battle in the United States. First, the push toward learning and knowing English, and *only* English, is formidable. It is evident to any observer of U.S. culture that participation in political, economic, social, and popular-culture sectors requires the ability to use English and to use it well. The 5-year-old who watches *Sesame Street* and Saturday morning cartoons can tell you that English is where the action is. It is the language of mass media, the language of toys and games, and the language spoken by authority figures in their lives, such as teachers. Adult arrivals encounter the same overwhelming dominance of English. For many, the preeminence of English in the United States is an amplification of the mass influence of English in their native countries, where U.S. culture and English-language media have penetrated the general and popular domains. Although some may settle in cultural enclaves with others from the native country, the benefits of knowing English are inescapable. The importance of English may be *especially* poignant for those who live in economically poor ethnic enclaves. From that vantage point, one can see most profoundly the disparity between the English-speaking mainstream and one's own immigrant community.

Immigrants seem to be well aware of the advantages of learning English. A 1979 nationally representative survey of U.S. residents of Mexican heritage found that more than 45% believed that it "improves employment benefits," and another nearly 23% believed that being bilingual in the United States brings about societal and community benefits and improved opportunities, including education.[9] For immigrants, being able to speak English can also be a key to being accepted by the dominant group and to feel as though they belong to the mainstream.[10] Being accepted and avoiding alienation is perhaps one of the biggest pulls toward English, especially for children and adolescents.

Charles Ryu arrived in the United States at the age of 17 and observed that among the Korean community in the United States, there is a prevailing belief that English proficiency affords a certain status not available to those with little or imperfect fluency. He comments:

> So among Koreans, language anxiety is very, very strong. If you speak good English, you tend to think you are better off than those that don't. And those who don't speak good English, are often envious of those who can. So it is there; we don't speak about it.[11]

Michael Feng, a Chinese American born and raised in New York, believes that in his high school, speaking English perfectly—fluently and without accent—was very important in being accepted by nonminority students. He had a friend who didn't speak "good English" and who had trouble being accepted by his American peers.[12]

Whereas knowing English may bring prestige and acceptance, speaking another language—especially a low-status language—can do the opposite. The negative consequences of speaking a heritage language can range from experiencing shame for being different to facing racist or xenophobic reactions in school, work, or community. To sound different is to be different, especially for visible minorities who have physical characteristics that signal them as part of a minority group. Once one is labeled an aberration and an outsider, gaining acceptance into the mainstream can be difficult. When these feelings are internalized by minority-language speakers, a natural reaction they experience is to distance themselves from being a minority and to attempt to be more like the majority. I documented a number of such cases among U.S. minority students, calling this phenomenon "ethnic evasion," and have described the negative effects these feelings have on interest in studying the heritage language and even willingness to speak it.[13] Essentially, those in ethnic evasion adopt negative mainstream society views of the heritage language as stigmatized, useless, and even subversive. Overcoming the psychological stigma erected by the power of English and the mantra of monolingualism can take many years, with some never shedding the shame they had come to associate with being minority-language speakers. Knowing English and knowing it well is of course important, but monolingualism is not the only path to achieving fluency in the language, a point missed by those who see English and English only as the sole path.

Limited Exposure to the Heritage Language

One way to understand how heritage languages are lost is to look at how little exposure to the language speakers may typically get. When we take a closer look at the daily language exposure of children who, on the surface, appear to live in heritage-language-rich environments, we see that the conditions are often not conducive to high levels of heritage language and literacy development. Let's look at the fictional case of Julio. He is 10 years old, lives in a Spanish-speaking community, attends a school with a bilingual education program, and has parents who speak Spanish at home. In many ways, this is the best-case scenario for maximum heritage language access, and one in which the language is likely to be developed. While Julio's case is a composite of a number of different descriptive accounts of the lives of bilingual children and schooling in bilingual education programs, it illustrates what we know about language exposure among these children.[14]

On a typical day the first thing Julio hears is his mother telling him in Spanish to wake up and to get ready for school. In the kitchen, he eats a bowl of his favorite cereal. He reads the back of the cereal box, while his younger sister is playing a Game Boy video game. "That's mine," Julio says to his sister. "In your dreams," Raquel responds in Spanish as she runs from the table. "OK, enough. It's time to go," Julio's mother tells them in Spanish.

Julio takes the bus to school, which is approximately two miles from their home. Waiting at the bus stop, Julio sees his best friend, David, and asks him whether he saw the new show on TV last night. The two boys speak to each other half in Spanish, half in English. They have been friends ever since the first grade, when David's family moved into the neighborhood. At first, they spoke only Spanish with each other, but as their games, toys, and interest in television shows became increasing English oriented, English became the more convenient language to use to talk about them.

Julio and David are both in the same transitional bilingual education third-grade class. In kindergarten, the teacher spoke primarily Spanish and used English during music time, math time, and when the class played games in the school yard. In the first grade, the teacher spoke less Spanish, and taught math, science, and music in English. Last year, the day was divided in half, with English in the morning and Spanish in the afternoon. This year, the teacher speaks almost entirely in English and only speaks Spanish when students need clarification or further explanation, especially with those who are newly arrived from Mexico, South America, or Central America. Math, language arts, science, social studies/history, music, and art are all taught in English, and student work is done almost entirely in English. Next year, Julio and David will be "mainstreamed" into classes with other English-fluent students.[15]

After school, Julio takes the bus home and finishes his homework as quickly as possible so he can watch his favorite cartoons. After an hour and a half of schoolwork, both Julio and Raquel gather in front of the TV at precisely 4:30 p.m., when an English-language cartoon about a team of superheros comes on. At 5, they watch *Lightning Man*, also in English, as he tries to elude his arch enemy and reach the Golden City. At 5:30 p.m., English-language *Looney Tunes* comes on for an hour. At 6:30, Julio and Raquel's mother returns home from work and they help prepare dinner. After dinner, the two children help clean up and watch a couple more hours of TV—again in English—before heading to bed.

On a typical day, Julio is exposed to more than 10 hours of English and less than 4 hours of Spanish. The 10 hours spent in English include both conversational language *as well as* academic language and literacy in school. The far fewer hours in Spanish consists entirely of conversation among family and friends, and limited instruction by the teacher, but after the first or second grade, *no exposure to literacy*. What results is an imbalance: high levels of English-language proficiency, academic knowledge, and literacy-related skills, and primarily oral proficiency in Spanish, with little academic knowledge or literacy ability in that language. Even in this apparent best-case scenario where a child has a parent who speaks the heritage language, has peers who are bilingual, and attends a bilingual education program, the best that the child can do is to develop conversational Spanish, with English quickly becoming his or her better language and the one he or she prefers to use.

Limited Opportunities to Learn the Heritage Language

Another reason for widespread language loss is the lack of efforts in U.S. schools designed to help students develop their heritage language. Existing heritage language programs are of three types: community language schools, "maintenance" bilingual education programs, and foreign-language native-speaker courses. In some communities, secular or parochial private language schools exist to teach the language. Generally, these private community schools are supported by parents who want their children to learn the heritage language and to gain some familiarity with the heritage culture. In Tucson, Arizona, 50 students gather each Saturday for 4 hours of language lessons and to participate in cultural activities, such as singing, dancing, martial arts, or painting. Parents bring their children for their classes, some leaving to run errands while others remain at the school to chat with other waiting parents or to help in leading cultural lessons. After 2 hours of language lessons, students gather in the main hall and on the playground to take part in cultural activities, some learning to draw with brush pens, some singing folk songs, while others practice kung fu moves and spar with one another. In general, these "after school schools" and "Saturday schools" attempt to teach students some rudiments of the heritage language and sometimes serve as child care.[16]

These efforts generally face formidable obstacles.[17] First, such schools are often crippled by inadequate resources and must operate with untrained teachers and textbooks inappropriate for students raised in an American setting. Teachers are sometimes mothers or community members, and texts are often outdated. Second, students themselves are oftentimes reluctant to attend these extra hours of schooling while their peers have free time (see Chapter 4 for a further discussion).

A second type of program designed to foster the heritage language is a form of bilingual education called "developmental," "maintenance," or "late-exit" bilingual education, which constitutes a small percentage of existing bilingual education programs in the United States.[18] These programs are designed to help students become fluent and literate in two languages by maintaining and developing the native language while students learn English. By the time students exit the program, they should have both conversational and academic facility in two languages. Long established in other countries, these programs appear to produce consistently good results when the proper support and resources are available.

Despite public perception, however, the majority of existing bilingual education programs in the United States are not of this type and are *not* designed to preserve the native language. Nearly all bilingual education programs are of the type Julio attends, the "transitional" or "early exit" variety. Transitional programs have two primary goals—to teach students English and to help students maintain progress in their academic subjects—stopping the use of the heritage language as soon as students are proficient in English. Recall that in the case of Julio, the teacher used Spanish only up through the third grade, assuming that students reach grade-level ability in English by that time. In fourth grade, Julio will be in a classroom where the only language used for instruction is English and Spanish will disappear altogether from his formal schooling.

The third type of heritage language education is the foreign-language native-speaker course. Some high schools and colleges with large numbers of heritage language speakers have instituted separate native-speaker sections to distinguish the needs of these students from the traditional foreign-language learner. The different linguistic profiles of heritage- and traditional foreign-language learners make it problematic for both sets of students to enroll in the same course. While heritage language speakers may be able to speak the language quite well, these students typically have limited literacy and knowledge of grammatical conventions in written language. In contrast, the more traditional foreign-language learner begins study with little or no ability to speak the language, and unlike many native-speaker students, often finds learning to communicate orally the greatest challenge. Native-speaker programs have been in existence for a number of years and appear to be growing. Language-teaching organizations, such as the American Council for the Teachers of Foreign Languages and the Modern Language Association, have for many years addressed issues related to teaching native speakers at their annual conferences. In fact, in 1995, instructors in Spanish for Native Speakers programs created their own annual conference. Yet, despite these indications that heritage language learners are receiving more attention in the teaching profession, such courses are far from being systematically implemented throughout secondary and higher education institutions.[19]

Parental and School Misconceptions about Language Learning

Parents are in many ways gatekeepers to the heritage language: Whether parents speak to their children in the native language; the attitudes parents hold about maintenance of the language; whether opportunities are sought out for the child to be exposed to or to formally study the language; and whether parents provide reading materials in the home or model uses of literacy (such as recreational reading and letter writing); all may all have an impact on whether and to what extent the language is retained by children.[20]

The first possible exposure to the heritage language for any child is in the home before the child reaches school age. Unfortunately, many immigrant parents operate under the false assumption that speaking a language other than English at home will hamper English-language learning and school success. As a result, parents may insist on speaking only English at home, even though the parents themselves are limited-English speakers and may have difficulty communicating with their children using the language.

Why do parents make the decision to speak only English? Some parents may want to protect their children from the discrimination they face as imperfect speakers of English. Parents who are ridiculed, ignored, or treated condescendingly because of their halting or heavily accented speech understandably want their children to avoid the same derision. This, together with the fear that passing on the native language will somehow limit English language learning motivates many parents to "safeguard" their children from this dreaded prospect.

Raised in Hawaii, Will Hao recalled that when he was a child, his father discouraged him from learning pidgin English, a dialect of English and their heritage language. His father wanted none of his seven children to speak the dialect and urged his children to "learn the best English we could."[21] Victor Merina, who immigrated to the United States from the Philippines as a child, recalled that his parents discouraged the children from learning Tagalog, due in part to the many incidents when they or their children were taunted because of their nonnative English. Victor recalled,

> They didn't want us to learn Tagalog or a dialect from their islands, which is called Ivatan. At first they spoke both dialects at home with my sister and I. But after the incidents of language in school [in which we were made fun of], they made a conscious decision not to mix the languages. So they didn't speak any Tagalog to my sister or I when we were growing up.[22]

It is precisely because immigrant parents know the value of English that they decide to raise their children monolingually, often not seeing the long-term drawbacks of not passing on the heritage language.

Parents may come to the conclusion to limit the heritage language at home on their own, or they may be prompted by school administrators and teachers who believe in this flawed educational strategy. The Villegas family immigrated to a town outside of San Francisco and wanted to find a academically rigorous school for their youngest daughter, Diana, eventually deciding on a private academy in the adjacent, affluent town. Before school started, Mr. and Mrs. Villegas brought their daughter to meet her new kindergarten teacher. Without hesitation, the teacher firmly advised the Villegases against teaching Diana to read and write in Spanish, and encouraged them to speak English at home to avoid creating "a conflict" that would result in Diana's having problems in school. The Villegases did not question the teacher's advice and began to speak only English in the home. It wasn't long before the effects of language shift became apparent. During a visit from her Spanish-only-speaking grandparents about a year later, both the grandparents and Diana's parents realized how limited Diana's Spanish was when she couldn't communicate effectively using only Spanish. Mr. and Mrs. Villegas briefly considered transferring Diana to a school with a maintenance bilingual education program, but could not find one that met their needs.[23]

Professor Ortiz, a higher education administrator originally from Puerto Rico recalled what teachers told him about his child's education: "We were requested to speak more English at home or to stop speaking Spanish at home, and speak English for the sake of her [his daughter] learning the language." When she was a young girl, Mrs. Escobar, now a school administrator herself, recalled teachers telling her to speak only English now that she was in the United States (even though she was from Puerto Rico, a U.S. commonwealth). She reflected that "the message that we got loud and clear was the fact that little value was placed on our language and culture throughout my elementary education."[24]

Community and Peer Influences

Beyond the immediate family, the heritage language community may also serve to encourage or discourage the development of the language. Children living outside close-knit heritage communities seldom come in contact with institutions that use and value the heritage language. Having little access to places such as church or temple where high-status members of the community—such as religious leaders—use the heritage language means fewer opportunities for a child to hear it spoken for authentic and important purposes and to see the language as a valuable asset.

Peers also have enormous influence over our opinions and actions, and may determine, for example, the importance we place on knowing the heritage language and the openness we feel toward learning it. Consider the influence our co-workers have on our dress, attitudes, and behaviors. We tend to internalize some of the values and beliefs of those whom we consider successful or well liked, and may adjust the way we talk and interact with others accordingly. The same forces are at work with peer influence on heritage language learning. Encountering a peer group that we consider desirable and that also happens to use and value the heritage language encourages us to improve our proficiency in that language, to use it more often, and to identify ourselves as a heritage language speaker. For children and adolescents, peer influence may be particularly strong and the presence or absence of such heritage language groups determines to a large extent whether the language is seen as an asset or a liability.

Julie grew up speaking Japanese with her family at home but was never interested in developing her heritage language ability until, in junior high school, she befriended a group of girls from Japan who moved to the United States as a result of their parents' company transfer. As recent arrivals, these students were interested in Japanese teen culture and participated in activities typical of Japanese teens, such as reading serial comic books and listening to pop music. Being around these girls and wanting to be accepted by the group, Julie also became interested in reading comic books and listening to Japanese music and soon became an avid reader of comic books and poured over Japanese lyrics to learn the latest songs. Being a member of this close-knit social circle gave her exposure to the language she would otherwise not have had, and she grew to see speaking and reading Japanese as necessary skills in her daily interactions. She considered being highly proficient in Japanese an asset for relating to and being a full-fledged member of this social circle.[25]

THE MYTH OF LANGUAGE GHETTOS

The rule, then, is for immigrant tongues to disappear over generations and to stop developing even within one's lifetime. But why does it seem as though immigrant languages linger in the United States? When we drive through immigrant neighborhoods such as Little Havana in Miami, Koreatown in Los Angeles, and Chinatown in San Francisco, we get the sense that these are stagnant linguistic neighborhoods where only Spanish, Korean, or Chinese is spoken generation after generation.[26]

How do we resolve this paradox of the perpetual language ghetto with evidence that children such as Rick, Julio, and Diana never develop much ability in their heritage language as they learn English?

Influx of New Immigrants

One key to understanding this apparent contradiction is to look more closely at migration patterns among immigrants and their children. These patterns show that successive generations rarely live in the same enclave community. That is, the children and grandchildren of immigrants usually move out of the enclave and are replaced by new immigrant families.

It is helpful to understand just how these ethnically concentrated communities get started and perpetuated. When adult immigrants arrive, especially without significant financial resources or English skills, they tend to gravitate toward communities where they are likely to get assistance in settling into their new surroundings. These communities not only provide the new arrival with the ability to survive without significant English ability (at least initially), but also may provide formal or informal networks for getting a job, finding housing, and navigating governmental agencies. In fact, having personal contacts in the new community may be critical in determining the level of adjustment newcomers reach by providing them with resources such as housing, transportation, and access to information about U.S. culture and society.[27] Anyone who has traveled abroad may be familiar with American expatriate communities offering some of these same supports to those trying to adjust to a new setting.

The limitations of immigrant communities—as institutionally established and extensive as they may be—propel those who are able to gain some level of acceptance outside of the immigrant community to look for resources beyond these neighborhoods. That is why second and later generations are less likely to live as adults and raise their own families in such communities, especially since the typical immigrant enclave tends to be comparatively socioeconomically depressed. As these children of immigrants become English proficient and educated, they move to other areas with more opportunities and higher social status.

As families move out, new arrivals take their place. The impression that heritage languages linger in immigrant families generation after generation is perpetuated in part by the influx of these new immigrants, who come in steady streams or larger waves (as with refugee resettlements).[28] This infusion, consistent or sporadic, creates the image of linguistically stagnant neighborhoods. However, when immigrants stop entering in significant numbers—as in the case of German immigration after World War I—enclaves tend to dissipate, and with them, the non-English languages used in them.

New Dialects of English and "Codeswitching"

A second factor contributing to the illusion of long-term immigrant language perpetuation is the emergence of English dialects influenced by languages other than English. Chicano English and Vietnamese English are only two examples of the many varieties of English that have emerged as a result of the influence of non-English languages.[29] Although these dialects are controversial in political arenas, linguists have documented these and other varieties of English and consider them logical language systems governed by definable rules, just as any other language system—including the standard English used in American media and schools. Some of these varieties of English are influenced by more recent immigrant languages and may appear as though they are simply amalgams of English and the heritage language. In fact, speakers of nonstandard dialects are often bidialectical, able to use a different dialect when the context warrants. When the standard dialect is called for, the speaker is able to shift linguistic gears and to use it in appropriate ways. And as these individuals attend school and find work out of the enclave, usage of the nonstandard dialect tends to be reserved primarily for speaking with family and heritage language community members, whereas standard English is used in most other settings.

We should also keep in mind that, as many linguists have pointed out, no one language or dialect is inherently better or worse than others. Judgments about what is "correct" and what is "good English" are based on social and political considerations, not linguistic ones. Therefore, the "standard" dialect is typically the language variation spoken by the group(s) that hold political, economic, and social power. We may hold opinions about who sounds better to us—a New Yorker or a Texan—but as long as language systems are rule-governed, they are all equally "correct." Yet, people have difficulty accepting this. A recent *New York Times* article described how a linguist at West Virginia University spoke to a group of students in the state and was condemned by community members for legitimizing nonstandard dialects. The linguist's basic message to the students was that dialects are innately neither good nor bad, and that the students should not be ashamed of their Appalachia dialect. After the talk, he and his superiors received angry letters from the community asking for his resignation.[30]

That is not to say that people don't mix languages in conversation. When people of similar language backgrounds communicate, it is sometimes useful to draw on more than one language and many do so naturally and without much thought. Linguists call this "codeswitching."[31] For instance, a pair of friends, Eduardo and Raul, both bilingual in English and Spanish, are watching a TV show one afternoon. One remarks, "*Mataron muchos* ducks" [They killed a lot of ducks] and "*¿Qué pasó?* [What happened?] It crashed?"[32] The two continue their exchange using both languages perhaps even without realizing they are codeswitching.[33] Codeswitching has been used throughout the ages and there are many examples in religious and literary texts. For instance, in published 16th-century prayers, both German and Latin are used in the same texts, and in Tolstoy's *War and Peace,* he alternates between French and Russian.[34]

Are these indications that a speaker has failed to learn any one language well, requiring switching between the two to get a message across? No. What linguistic research shows is that codeswitching is often done for reasons that are political, social, economic, or a combination of these, to establish or reinforce identification or allegiance or for other specific purposes. For instance, codeswitching can forge links with a particular community or social group, much like that done when one displays a bumper sticker of an alma mater or wears a baseball cap with a favorite team's logo.

The mixing of languages may also involve what linguists term *borrowing,* where words from one language are adapted and used as part of the second language, eventually becoming an integrated part of that language. English speakers "anglicize" words all the time, as do speakers of other languages. A Spanish speaker might say "*Ay te wacho* [I'll be seeing you]" using a modified form of the English word *watch* in this case.[35] This is a natural occurrence when languages come into contact. Sometimes borrowing is used for convenience when words for ideas and things don't exist in a given language. It is easier for me to use the Cantonese names for dishes served at Chinese brunch—dim sum—than to try to describe them in English when speaking to another regular dim sum–goer. It's quite natural and far more efficient. In this case, it is not a sign of my limited ability to use either language, but perhaps of the limitations of any one language for all things.

Confusing Non-English Speakers with Bilinguals

A third factor contributing to the myth of perpetual language barrios has to do with the lack of American acceptance of the additive nature of language learning. Monolingualism in the United States is so common and true bilingualism so rare that it is difficult for the public to grasp the concept of "additive bilingualism," the learning of a second language *without* losing the first. We can see this in numerous instances of media outcry when a language other than English is used for public discourse, which to many is an indication of resistance to English. The usual reaction from the accusers is that "this is America," and everyone should speak English. When the "offenders" respond that they are in fact bilingual and able to operate in two languages, the "accuser" has a difficult time understanding how this can be the case.

In 1999, the town of El Cenizo, Texas, declared Spanish its official language. Outraged that a language other than English would be given this distinction, two Albuquerque, New Mexico, disk jockeys called the El Cenizo city hall to complain. When an official explained that the decision was made so that Spanish could be used *in addition to English* to help those not yet fluent in English to get social services, the DJs told the clerk to "go back to Mexico."[36]

This exchange illustrates the often-made assumption—especially involving low-status languages—that anyone speaking a non-English language must not be competent in English. This is certainly possible, but not probable. It is much more likely that non-English-language speakers are bilingual. How do we know this? According to the 1990 Census, of those who speak a language other than English, more than 90% also speak English to some degree, and about 75% reported that they speak English "well" or "very well." They may not be fluent, but clearly nearly all *have* learned English to some level and an overwhelming majority operate easily in the language (see Chapter 2 for further discussion of adult immigrant English ability).

I've discussed in this chapter the short lives of immigrant languages, some of the causes of language loss, and the myth of perpetual language ghettoes. Why should we care whether heritage languages are lost? Are there benefits to being bilingual? In the following chapter, I will address these two important questions and discuss current support for dual-language learning.

CHAPTER 4

Why Promote Heritage Languages?

In the United States, heritage languages are disappearing from families and communities at a rapid rate, and the opportunities to become bilingual are severely limited. But why should we—as a nation—care? Why does it matter that the children of immigrants lose the native language and don't become bilingual or biliterate? Some have argued that these losses are simply the price immigrants families must pay for living in the United States.

This high price, however, is not paid by immigrants alone. The negative consequences of language loss and the benefits of preserving heritage languages have far-reaching implications for the individual and larger U.S. society alike. For this reason, how heritage languages are treated in this country is an important national public policy issue.

In this chapter, I discuss the likely rewards of heritage-language promotion and the disadvantages of forfeiting this linguistic resource. I also consider the current level of support for the two paths to bilingualism—foreign- and heritage language development—showing that little is currently being done to support the latter despite potential benefits.

BENEFITS OF HERITAGE LANGUAGE DEVELOPMENT

Developing the heritage language has two major sets of advantages for children and adolescents. First, for students still learning English, taking advantage of the native language can speed the acquisition of English and make it possible to continue learning school subjects while still improving English. Second, students who are already fluent in English and who maintain and develop their heritage language can become bilingual and biliterate, which carries personal advantages as well as important potential contributions to society. I elaborate on both sets of benefits in the next section.

Advantages for English-Language Learning and
Academic Development

The strategy of forsaking the heritage language to improve English learning is based upon the widely held myth that knowing one language will hamper the learning of a second. This myth is based perhaps on the popular notion that individuals have a limited capacity for knowing language. Many believe that our brains are like our stomachs: To have room for dessert, we can't overeat. Just like an expanding balloon, some believe, our brains can only hold so much, and if we fill it too fully with the heritage language, there will be no room for English. This misconception leads many parents and teachers to advocate arresting development of the native language to leave ample room for the new language.

Language learning research actually tells us the opposite. Not only do we appear to have infinite capacity for language learning, but knowing one language may help a learner pick up a second better and faster because it means not having to start from scratch. Just as the badminton player learning tennis will not have to relearn the functions of a racket or the notions of serves and volleys, a learner proficient in one language can, when learning a second, often build upon what he or she already knows from having learned a first.

Let's take the case of Rita, a native English speaker, who wants to learn French. Rita is a news junky and reads the newspaper daily. Luckily for Rita, her neighbor is a French speaker who also happens to keep up with current events. When they get together for coffee, Rita's neighbor, Jane, speaks to her about the day's headline stories *in simplified French* and Rita is able to understand because she has already read the paper that day *in English* and has the background information to make sense of the new French words she hears. In other words, Rita is picking up new labels—in French—for old concepts learned in English. Her ability to read in English— her first language—allows her to gain information to better understand (and learn) the new language. After a few months, Jane lends Rita her French-language newspapers and Rita begins to read them. Because Rita has read so many newspapers in the past in English, and journalistic stories in the United States and France are generally written in the same style, she knows that the first paragraph usually contains the most important information or the "lead," that some sections of the paper contain news stories and other parts contain editorials, that the sports scores are generally found in the sports section, and so forth. Rita has extensive knowledge of literacy conventions that help her begin to make sense of the French newspaper.[1]

The same capacity to draw upon prior experience and knowledge is also available for children learning English in schools. What students know in one language can improve their learning in two ways. First, having background information helps English language learning. Learning about a topic is easiest and quickest in one's strongest language, in this case, a student's native language. Armed with this background information, when students hear that topic talked about (or written about) in a new language, they are able to understand more than if they had no familiarity with the topic beforehand. Understanding more of the new language means that the learner will pick up the language that much faster. In Rita's case, her background knowledge of current events learned through her native language, English, helped her better understand what Jane said to her in French, which in turn spurred her learning of French. Second, having background knowledge gained through the first language allows students to learn subject matter more effectively in English. If you already know some information about a particular topic (and can better understand the language of instruction as a result), you can better understand not only the new language but also the related *content* being taught. Since Rita already knows the basic issues related to air pollution in the United States, for instance, she is well prepared to hear Jane speak in French about the issue in European contexts. She will not be able to understand everything said, but will be able to pick up more than if she knew nothing about the subject prior to their conversation.

If students don't have background knowledge in their first language, the alternative is to simultaneously learn new material while also trying to learn the English labels for those brand-new concepts. Doing so would be far more difficult and time consuming. In fact, research shows that for English language learners, building background knowledge in the first and stronger language while learning English is the most efficient and effective means to ensure that English is acquired and school subjects are learned well. This is the strategy behind bilingual education.

As Rita's example also shows, background information makes learning to read and write in a new language easier as well. Children reading a book in English for the first time, for example, can apply many of the same strategies they use when reading in their heritage language. Even people learning to read in a language with a different writing system benefit from being able to read in their first, as we can see in the following scenario.[2]

Mikhail and Andrei, both recent arrivals from Russia, enter the third grade.[3] Mikhail had lived in Moscow and had attended school since age 6. Andrei had lived in a small farming village and had not yet begun to attend school because he was needed to work on the farm. Both boys are placed in the same third-grade class when they arrive in the United States. Because Mikhail already knows how to read in Russian, he picks up a book and knows, for instance, that words make up sentences, which in turn make up paragraphs, chapters, and so on. He knows that words in his textbook that are in bold or underlined are those that comprehension questions are likely to be asked about or those that students will be tested on. He knows that the first sentence in each section of the book gives a summary or introduces the topic of the text that follows. He knows that when he comes across a word he doesn't know, he should keep reading, since he can usually guess the meaning from the clues in the rest of the sentence or paragraph. Mikhail can bring all this knowledge to bear when he begins to read in English, even though the two languages have different orthographies, or writing systems. Andrei, who didn't learn to read in Russian, doesn't have this information about stories and textbooks that Mikhail picked up from having attended school. There is little doubt that Mikhail will learn to read in English far more quickly than Andrei and be able to learn in English far sooner.

Let's consider another case of how background information can help oral-language and literacy development as well as subject matter learning. Imagine that you've lived all your life in the United States and have worked as a bookkeeper for 20 years. Ed McMahon appears at your door and announces that you've won the 10-million-dollar Publisher's Clearinghouse Sweepstakes. You quit your job and move to Greece, where you've always wanted to live. Unfortunately, you don't speak any Greek. You've always dreamed of becoming a psychologist and enroll at the local junior college in Athens to begin your studies. During the class sessions, you are so lost that, not only do you not understand any of the Greek the instructor is speaking, you've missed out on the content of the course. You stick it out for the entire semester, but by the time you begin to understand a few words in the language at the end of the semester, you've fallen so far behind in your knowledge of psychology that you can't move ahead to next semester's course. You have no choice but to repeat the first course. The second time around, however, you get smart and secure help in two ways. First, before the course begins again, you read three basic psychology textbooks *in English* that cover the prerequisite information for the course. Second, you hire a bilingual student also taking the course to give you a review of the professor's lectures after each class meeting *in English*. This second time through you understand far more, and although you're still not comprehending all the instructor's discussions, you are getting by. Getting background information through your first language made it easier to understand the second language *and* helped you survive academically in your studies. Building background knowledge through the native language has these two important benefits for both children and adults trying to learn new content and a new language.[4]

Bilingualism Has Benefits

For the individual. Learning English while maintaining the heritage language is perhaps the easiest and most efficient way to achieve bilingualism, and being bilingual carries advantages in many domains. First, for children, bilingual ability may improve school performance. In the mid-1980s, two separate studies examined academic achievement among monolingual and bilingual high school seniors. In one study, the researchers found that bilingual students of Hispanic/Latino heritage were better readers in English and had higher academic aspirations than those who were Hispanic/Latino but monolingual in either English or Spanish. This suggests that those who develop their heritage language and know English well do better in school than those who leave the heritage language behind. A second study found nearly the same thing: Latino students who were able to speak both Spanish and English had high educational attainment and expectations. Moreover, some psychologists have found evidence that bilinguals have more creativity and better problem-solving skills than monolinguals. These researchers suggest that bilinguals have an advantage because they have more than one way of thinking about a given concept, making them more "divergent" thinkers and more effective problem solvers.[5]

There are also cultural and social advantages to being bilingual. Being able to communicate in two languages means having access to multiple sources of information, resources that have been dubbed "social capital" or "funds of knowledge." These additional avenues for assistance and knowledge may come from interactions with family and community members who may, for instance, supply important advice and life lessons. Being able to communicate with parents in their stronger or sole language can also minimize the generational gap that is often exacerbated by language differences (more on this below).[6]

Being bilingual carries economic advantages as well. Those fluent in two languages tend to earn more and have more career options. Latinos in Florida, for example, who speak English very well and who also speak Spanish have annual median incomes about 20% higher than Latinos who speak only English. Those in the Spanish-rich communities of Miami–Dade County make 50% more than monolingual employees, according to one study (also see below).[7] Although not all communities have the same level of bilingualism found in Miami, demographic trends show a growing number of language-minority families and students entering what were once largely monolingual regions, due in large part to growth in immigration.[8]

For society. The U.S. government has long recognized the need for bilingualism among its citizenry. The creation of the Defense Language

Institute for foreign-language teaching, the establishment of the Commission on Foreign Languages and International Studies by former president Jimmy Carter, and the publication of the widely cited book criticizing Americans' monolingualism by former senator Paul Simon of Illinois called *The Tongue-Tied American* demonstrate the awareness at least since the 1970s of the nation's language deficiencies.[9]

There are at least three ways society benefits from bilingualism. First, the United States garners advantages by having citizens who have linguistic (and perhaps cultural) savvy to negotiate with international business clients. The Spanish-speaking market in the United States and Latin America is large and growing. Kelly Cunningham, who worked as a research manager for the San Diego Regional Chamber of Commerce, pointed out that "[i]n addition to a quarter of our population being Hispanic, Latin America has a huge economic impact on us. We export $3.8 billion worth of goods to Mexico and $386 million to Central and South America." He also noted that Mexicans spend $2 billion in retail stores and $2 billion on services in the United States, which makes U.S. and Mexican "economies and cultures vitally intertwined."[10] According to U.S. International Trade Administration's tourism industries figures, Latin American tourism, including those from the Caribbean, Central and South America, and Mexico, has risen a remarkable 31% between 1990 and 1997, compared with a 21% increase in overall international tourist arrivals to the United States. In 1997, that amounted to 13 million visitors, the largest group entering the United States for travel. Travelers spent $18 billion in 1997 and generated an estimated 259,000 full-time U.S. jobs.[11]

A 1998 article in *Hispanic Business* magazine highlighted the difficulty businesses had in finding bilinguals and biliterates, a shortage that ultimately hurts foreign trade, tourism, and international banking. For instance, the Latin American headquarters of Visa International in Miami can't find bilingual employees who are able to give business presentations without making grammatical errors. The managers of a $20 million export company has to check carefully over letters written by bilingual sales people because of past inaccuracies, and Ceridian Performance Partners, a company with a large telemarketing center, has trouble finding a market researcher who can speak and write both Spanish and English well. These businesses operate in Miami, where about 75% of the residents are Latino. It is also a city that conducts 30% of all U.S. trade with South America and 43% with Central America. As a senior vice president for human resources at Visa's Latin American operations notes: "It's difficult to find true bilinguals. Most are mediocre bilinguals."[12]

It's not surprising, then, that those who are bilingual and biliterate earn more as employees in sales, customer relations, and public services, among other industries. The *San Diego Union-Tribune* reported in 2000 that bilinguals who speak Spanish or are fluent in Tagalog or other Asian languages in the San Diego area can expect to earn an additional $45 to $200 a month depending on the type of work and employer policy.[13] Steve Laughrin-Sacco, co-director of the Center of International Business Education and Research at San Diego State University, observed that being able to communicate in the customer's native language can be vital. "If your competitor speaks Spanish or Chinese or Tagalog, he or she might get the business if you're dealing with that population, both abroad and at home."[14] These observations are consistent with research by Joshua Fishman and others who have found that bilingualism benefits economies in the United States and internationally.[15]

Second, the nation benefits politically by possessing a rich diplomatic and national security corps. The President's Commission on Foreign Language and International Studies pointed out the importance of bilingualism:

> The fact remains that the overwhelming majority of the world's population neither understands nor speaks English, and for most of those who learn English as a foreign language, it remains precisely that. Our vital interests are impaired by the fatuous notion that our competence in other languages is irrelevant. Indeed, it is precisely because of this nation's responsibilities and opportunities as a major power and as a symbol of ideals to which many of the world's people aspire that foreign languages, as a key to unlock the mysteries of other customs and cultures, can no longer be viewed as an educational or civic luxury.[16]

Since 1946, the U.S. government has operated the largest foreign-language school in the country, the Defense Language Institute, to develop multilingualism among military and other government personnel. As of 2000, the school, located in Monterey, California, has a faculty of more than 750 and an enrollment of 2,500, nearly all from the four branches of the U.S. military, the Department of Defense, and the Federal Bureau of Investigation. According to the school's Web site, it consists of "1,000 classrooms and faculty offices, about 50 audio language labs and eight computer-enhanced language training labs." Additional resources include "more than 5,000 foreign television programs and films, in excess of 80,000 volumes in more than 40 languages and hundreds of foreign language newspapers and periodicals."[17]

This substantial investment in building a multilingual international corps is not surprising when we learn that even the Central Intelligence Agency has had "difficulty meeting its needs for critical language skills, even in commonly taught languages such as Spanish."[18] While the President's Commission on Foreign Language and International Studies suggested increased support for foreign-language programs, it also made a point to recognize the need to preserve heritage languages. The report stated: "The melting pot tradition that denigrates immigrants' maintenance of their skill to speak their native tongue still lingers, and this unfortunately causes linguistic minorities at home to be ignored as a potential asset."[19]

Third, the country gains educationally by stemming the shortage of foreign-language teachers, especially in the less common languages in the United States such as Farsi, Chinese, and Russian. In 1988, a survey was conducted of the 50 U.S. states and the District of Columbia to gauge the availability of foreign-language teachers.[20] The survey found a severe shortage of teachers especially at the elementary level, in rural areas, and in small school districts. More than 57% of states and the District of Columbia noted a shortage at one level or another, and 69% predicted a shortage in 5 years. Although a more recent survey is not available, the increase in foreign-language enrollment in the past 10 years (see the section "Foreign-language programs" later in this chapter), especially in less commonly taught languages, makes it likely that the shortage continues.

A related problem is the lack of bilingual teachers to work with students still learning English. Regardless of one's position on the hotly contested issue of bilingual education, it makes sense that teachers with bilingual ability have an added language asset to help students who enter the classroom speaking the same non-English language. Bilingual teachers can help students adjust to the new learning environment and culture so that students will feel more comfortable learning in English. The shortage of teachers with dual-language ability is stark, as evidenced by the ratio of bilingual teachers to students in California, shown in Table 4.1.

Just as we see basic math teachers with additional expertise in calculus and physics as important assets, so too are teachers fluent in other languages. In addition to helping students still learning English, bilingual teachers may be able to teach foreign languages to English monolingual students or to assist the school in communicating with parents to encourage participation in their children's education.

CONSEQUENCES OF HERITAGE LANGUAGE LOSS

In addition to the real benefits that accrue from heritage language development, there are also serious negative consequences to losing the language, including the emergence of an intergenerational language gap, the lack of acceptance by members of the heritage community, and the formidable task of reclaiming the language.

TABLE 4.1. Ratio of Bilingual Teachers to Students With Limited Proficiency in English, California (Olsen, 1997)

Child's Home Language	Teacher-Student Ratio
Spanish	1:81
Cantonese	1:108
Vietnamese	1:662
Hmong	1:1,113
Khmer	1:4,129
Cambodian	1:21,000+

One of the most serious hardships resulting from language loss is the conflict that emerges between parent and child, and between child and heritage community. When a child does not speak the heritage language and parents only have limited English ability, a gulf is created beyond the usual generational gap. Erika is a Korean American who only understands a little Korean, and explains the gap this way:

> It is frustrating when I'm speaking with my parents and we can't fully comprehend what we're trying to say to each other. I hate it when I eat dinner with my parents and they always carry on their own conversation that I can only half understand. Yet, they complain that we don't eat as a family enough. I hate having something to say but not being able to say it.[21]

Frustration and anger may result from these attempts to communicate. For instance, parents may address their teenage children using simple language normally reserved for a young child because that is the level of language the teenager can understand. Encouragements to "eat your food" and to "pick up after yourself" can be demeaning and frustrating for teenagers who see such admonishments as a lack of recognition of their maturity. At the same time, children may lack the words in the heritage language to explain behavior or opinions, and must bluntly state their views, sometimes offending parents and grandparents who see such direct talk as disrespectful.[22]

The impact of such language gaps should not be underestimated. Tension, frustration, and even fistfights have resulted from miscommunication, unintentional slights, and inability to convey even simple messages, undermining the parent-child relationship and limiting the assistance parents could provide in a wide range of matters. This is confounded by the inability to turn to community institutions and resources that may serve similar functions. Without knowledge of the language, entry into the heritage community can be limited. Those who don't speak the community language may be considered outsiders who lack one of the most salient symbols of group membership.

Another drawback of language loss is the difficulty encountered when trying to regain the heritage language. Finding schools offering the particular language or dialect spoken by the family may be quite difficult, especially for the less common foreign languages in the United States, such as Hmong, Arabic, and Croatian. Another obstacle to reclaiming the heritage language is the inability of "regular" foreign-language programs to meet the needs of native bilinguals who have different linguistic profiles from that of the typical foreign-language student. Heritage language speakers in such classes may get little attention from teachers who assume higher levels of proficiency from native speakers than they actually possess. Moreover, peers may resent native speakers who dominate class discussions and who may excel in oral language activities that the typical foreign-language learner finds more challenging. Finally, instruction and teaching materials may not be appropriate for these students, many of whom may have even advanced speaking ability but limited literacy. Encountering these adverse attitudes and getting inappropriate instruction lead many to give up learning the language altogether and abandon the potential to become bilingual and biliterate.[23]

SUPPORT FOR FOREIGN- VERSUS HERITAGE LANGUAGE PROGRAMS

Developing heritage languages and fostering bilingualism, then, result in both personal and societal advantages in economic, political, social, and educational sectors. Even a cursory look at the issue reveals that investment in heritage languages is a prudent and logical policy. How is it, then, that the general public is not more aware of the benefits of fostering heritage languages? This linguistic blind spot has, in part, grown out of the prevailing sentiment in the United States that heritage languages are a "problem" that needs to be solved, rather than a "resource" that can be cultivated and put to good use.[24]

Public Perception of Heritage Languages

Seen from this perspective, current U.S. policy toward heritage languages makes sense. What better way to guard against the potential problems posed by immigrant languages than to allow those languages to dissipate over time? By withholding recognition and support from heritage language preservation and development efforts, and by encouraging the use of only English through official and unofficial incentives and regulations, heritage languages vanish in two to three generations and the "problem" no longer exists.[25]

Ironically, as I discussed earlier in the chapter, research on the education of language-minority students paints a very different picture of the potential role of non-English languages. When minority languages are treated as *resources* rather than *problems,* heritage languages have the potential to benefit individuals and society alike. When non-English languages and bilingualism are developed, heritage-language-speaking children are more likely to become proficient in English, to succeed academically, and to contribute positively to the job force as adults, precisely the same goals held by language assimilationists. The bottom line is this: Rather than being a problem or a luxury, the heritage language is a necessity for the good of the individual as well as for larger society.

Enrollments in Foreign- and Heritage Language Programs

Despite the potential for a sizable bilingual population in the United States, however, policy governing language education has backed a different horse, that of foreign-language education. Some of the same students who are denied the opportunity to develop their heritage language during their formative years in school are, in junior high and high school, encouraged to become bilingual by learning a (new) "foreign" language. Popularity of foreign-language study continues to grow, but heritage-language-development efforts remain on the fringes as unsanctioned programs that rely almost solely on parental and community support. These negative public perceptions of heritage languages has led to disparities in support, evident in enrollment figures in foreign- and heritage language programs.

Foreign-language programs. From scanning the classified job ads in the newspaper, it is clear that in many fields, from professional domains to service sectors, bilingualism is a hot commodity.[26] This is a reality that has not escaped students enrolled in colleges and universities across the United States high schools, community colleges, and universities continue to expand their offerings, and there is a rapidly growing number of elementary schools adopting foreign-language programs.

In 1990, enrollment in modern foreign languages in U.S. colleges and universities reached a 30-year high, with a 30% increase from 1980. At the secondary school level, a survey conducted in 1994 by the American Council on the Teaching of Foreign Languages (ACTFL) found that more than 6 million students—33% of those in grades 7 through 12—were studying a language other than English.[27] Based on an analysis of the 1995 California Basic Education Data System information, the number of students enrolled in Japanese-language classes rose 861% in the 12-year period between 1982–83 and 1994–95, and Chinese enrollment increased 150% over that same period, with the most dramatic increase at the high school level.[28]

Figure 4.1 shows the percentage of elementary schools and high schools offering foreign-language programs in the United States. The overall figure for secondary schools has held steady over the previous 10 years, while there has been a nearly 10% increase at the elementary level since 1987.

These increases in foreign-language study coincide with the increased attention paid to foreign language competence beginning in the late 1970s and early 1980s. As I mentioned earlier, in 1979, a report commissioned by then president Jimmy Carter was released that examined foreign lan-

FIGURE 4.1. Percentage of Elementary and Secondary Schools Teaching Foreign Languages, 1997 (Adapted from Rhodes & Branaman, 1999)

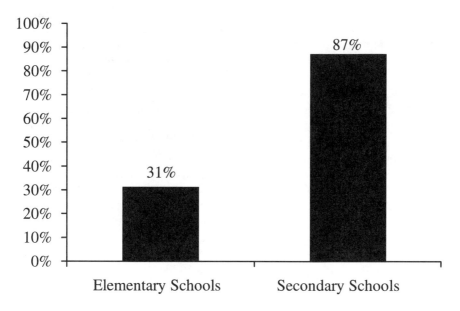

56 *"Why Don't They Learn English?"*

guage and international studies in the United States. The following year, former senator Paul Simon published his influential book, *The Tongue-Tied American*. Both lamented the lack of foreign-language and international experience among Americans in general, and emphasized the need to increase education efforts to prepare students for a borderless economic system and internationally oriented political consciousness. The commission report noted "America's scandalous incompetence in foreign languages" and provided detailed recommendations for adding federal support to expand educational efforts.[29]

Despite support for foreign-language education, such programs are doing little to curtail this "scandalous incompetence." Even though a growing number of students are taking foreign languages, at the college level, only 1 in 6 students continue after 2 years of study, a mere 15% of all foreign-language enrollment. This means that while a relatively large number of students learn the bare basics, few stick with it long enough to develop any true competence in a second language.[30]

Heritage language programs. The other route to bilingualism is heritage language development. Although 10% of the U.S. school-age population speak a heritage language to some degree, the number of programs to help these students develop their native language is minuscule compared with the number allowing foreign-language participation.

As I discussed in Chapter 3, there are three main types of heritage language development programs: (1) developmental bilingual education programs, (2) native speaker foreign/heritage language courses, and (3) heritage language schools. Developmental bilingual education programs, like other bilingual programs, have as their primary goal teaching students English. An added feature of developmental bilingual programs is that once students achieve English fluency and can perform at grade level in English, the development of their heritage language doesn't stop. Students learn nearly all their school subjects in English, but continue to improve their proficiency in the heritage language through, for instance, a Spanish-literature course or a Vietnamese-history class taught as part of the regular curriculum. In the 1994–95 school year, only about 9,800 students were enrolled in such federally funded programs in the United States, constituting a mere 0.3% of the limited English proficient students in the nation (see Figure 4.2). The percentage of students in such programs has held steady since 1991, indicating no growth in support for such efforts.[31]

A second type of program aimed at preserving and developing the heritage language is the foreign-language course tailored to native speakers. Most popular in Spanish programs in the United States, these native speaker courses are designed to meet the unique needs of students who may

FIGURE 4.2. Proportion of Limited English Proficient Students Enrolled in Title VII Federally Funded Developmental Bilingual Education Programs, 1994-95 (Macías, 1998. Retrieved February 12, 2000 from the World Wide Web: http://www.ncbe.gwu.edu/ncbepubs/seareports/96-97/f3.htm)

□ Total LEP Enrollment   ■ Proportion Enrolled in HL Courses

speak the language to some degree, but often have limited or no literacy in the language. Found primarily in high schools and colleges, these special course sections allow heritage language speakers to get the instruction and attention they need without adversely affecting the learning of traditional foreign language learners with whom they typically share a classroom, and vice versa. No reliable data is available on the effectiveness of these courses, but even if effective, these offerings come after 8 to 10 years of neglect and wasted opportunities for heritage language development.

The third type of maintenance and development program is the heritage language school. These schools generally operate as programs separate from and usually unconnected with mainstream day schools. Relatively little research has been done on these schools, which are typically privately operated after school, on the weekend, or both, some sponsored by church groups, some funded by student tuition. Most prevalent in middle- and upper-class communities, heritage language schools exist in far greater numbers for some language groups than others. For instance, there are national organizations of Chinese and Japanese language schools, but no such organization exists for Spanish and most other languages. The current support for heritage languages, even with these three types of heritage language programs, are clearly insufficient to meet the needs of the large heritage language population in the United States and cannot stem the loss of native languages.

We certainly don't want to eliminate current support for foreign-language programs. Rather, it seems to make sense—economically, politically, and educationally—to add additional support for heritage language programs. The current U.S. system pours resources into foreign-language programs in hopes of producing bilinguals without mending the holes in the system that allow heritage language speakers to lose their bilingual potential. Following this haphazard language policy seems contradictory at best, and at worst, wasteful and absurd. What is needed is both governmental recognition that the preservation of heritage languages is a national priority and financial backing to support its cultivation. Funding to create and maintain such programs in our public school systems is critical for any systematic programs to be implemented.

What if such governmental support were widely available? What types of programs are likely to work? In the following chapter, I discuss the characteristics of sound language learning programs and highlight selected promising approaches.

CHAPTER 5

How Can Heritage Languages Be Promoted?

One of the most memorable language lessons I've ever seen was one given by Father Guido Sarducci, a character portrayed by comedian Don Novello on *Saturday Night Live* during the 1970s. Sarducci made commentaries about daily and political events, and one of his best was a 15-minute current events and economics "lesson" that satirized the recession of the late 1970s.

Sarducci begins by showing a slide of then U.S. president Carter, noting that his favorite pastime is fishing and that his friends call him Jimmy. He then presents the well-known parallels between the presidencies of Abraham Lincoln and John F. Kennedy, followed by a parody, the fictional "Carter-Coolidge" coincidences. He draws several comical links between Carter and Coolidge's years in office, including the fact that both of their names begin with the letter *C*. He then launches into a chronicle of the late 1970s' economic woes by showing how many McDonald's Big Macs could be purchased in the decades preceding 1980, with fewer and fewer hamburgers remaining on the screen, until only one bite is left in 1980. The act ends with Sarducci warning Carter that if this trend continued, he would return to Georgia to take up fishing full time.[1]

What makes this a language lesson? The routine was performed *entirely* in Italian. Using cognates and visuals, Sarducci is able to communicate rather sophisticated subject matter—political satire—in a language that few, if any, of the members of the audience speak. Even more remarkable is how entertaining the commentary is to watch. In short, this skit contained two important components that researchers have identified as crucial for language learning. Sarducci (1) conveyed messages in a new language that were easy to understand, and (2) reinforced allegiance and group membership among audience members by building upon common knowledge and sentiments.

LANGUAGE EXPOSURE AND GROUP MEMBERSHIP

Let's take a look at each of these two critical language learning elements by discussing why each is important for heritage language development. Then, we will examine some classroom research that points the way to educational programs likely to foster heritage language learning.

The Language We Need

The first thing we need in order to learn a new language is substantial exposure to the language through either listening or reading.[2] Ideally, that exposure is in the form of interesting messages so captivating that learners are caught up in the understanding of those messages, rather than concentrating on picking apart the grammar or memorizing words. If this is the case, learners are likely to pick up large amounts of language and will do so effortlessly and unconsciously. When I show the Father Sarducci skit to my education students, they are not aware that they are picking up any Italian, although by the end of the 15-minute routine, many of them know how to say a number of Italian words used in the video, including "coincidence" and "fishing," words repeated several times in different contexts, with no definitions or any other direct instruction given on their pronunciation or meaning. With more exposure of this type, students gradually acquire much of the language they encounter.[3]

The Group Membership We Need

While researchers have looked quite extensively at the language exposure we need to learn a new language, a second set of factors that are equally important has received far less attention. These factors relate to "group membership," or the allegiances we feel with particular-language-speaking groups and the attitudes and feelings that flow from being associated with them. In other words, group membership is important because we tend to learn languages better when we feel like a member of the group of people who speak that language.[4]

This occurs, in part, because people make sense of the world by recognizing and creating social categories, and how we see ourselves is largely determined by the groups we see ourselves as belonging to.[5] When I ask my students as part of a class activity to describe themselves in 50 words or less, they inevitably define themselves according to the groups they belong to, such as "undergraduate/graduate student," "jazz lover," "education major," or "native of a certain city." Group membership carries consequences, both benefits and liabilities, in such things as status, prestige, and self-esteem, and we strive to identify with, and to be identified with, groups that we see as agreeable. Typically, students writing their 50-word bios will mention groups they see as positive or at least neutral, and avoid referring to those that are generally considered less desirable (e.g., "D-average student" or "Barry Manilow fan").

Although it is ultimately our own opinions that determine our group membership, our sense of belonging is influenced by a wide variety of factors such as the larger political climate, historical events, the type and level of that language's use in broader society, the interactions we have with different language and cultural groups, and the groups available for us to join, among other things. Because group membership is influenced by factors that are often out of our control, we may have constraints on the group memberships we can select from and ultimately choose. And even if we pick a certain group, these outside influences may prevent us from ever feeling wholly a member of that chosen group. In other words, there are group memberships that are imposed upon us by other people who categorize us differently from how we categorize ourselves, but who have more power. For instance, even though I may want to join the "surfer" group, the fact that I can't swim and that each time I step into the ocean, vivid memories of the movie *Jaws* flashes before my eyes, precludes that membership, regardless of how much I want to be part of that group. Laws of gravity—forces outside my control and more powerful than my will—prevent me from participating in the activities that are required for surfer club membership, dooming my chances for being accepted into that group.[6]

In terms of heritage language learning, language plays an important role as one of the most salient heritage group identifiers. Because of this, language learning is more likely to occur when we see the heritage group as desirable and we feel good about being associated with it.[7] As literacy researcher Frank Smith points out,

> [L]anguage gets so much attention because it is a primary way by which we establish our own identity and also the primary way by which we identify and categorize other people. It is perceived to be the core of everyone's identity.[8]

How Language and Group Membership Are Linked

How are language exposure and group membership related? The two are inextricably connected, as we can see in this case of Meg.[9]

Meg is 18 and a Japanese American born and raised in southern California. Her parents immigrated to the United States as adults, and while

Meg was growing up, her parents spoke Japanese at home to her and her two brothers. From kindergarten through high school, Meg continued to speak to her parents in Japanese but never learned to read and write the language, and after just a few years of attending elementary school, she became fluent in English and was a better speaker of English than of Japanese.[10]

At school, few of her friends, classmates, or teachers spoke Japanese, and since she wanted to be regarded as just like her English-only speaking friends, Meg saw little need to know Japanese. After all, the people around her and those she wanted to associate with were all English speaking. She had little exposure to Japanese other than from her parents, and although she attended a community Japanese school, she didn't have many friends there and had no desire to improve her Japanese. Her proficiency remained at about the same level throughout her childhood and adolescent years.

This all changed when Meg started college. She quickly became close friends with a cousin who was fluent in both English and Japanese and also befriended a number of her cousin's friends, who were also bilingual. When the group got together, they would often use both languages to socialize—to talk about school, work, movies, and a host of other topics. Being around these friends and hearing them discuss a range of subjects beyond what she typically heard at home helped Meg learn how to talk about topics outside of home and family. She also became increasingly interested in improving her own Japanese reading and writing ability so that she could be more like the other women in the group who often read Japanese fashion and pop culture magazines. The more Meg was exposed to the language, the more she learned and felt a part of the group. The more she felt like a part of the group, the more she wanted to learn and the more exposure she sought. She eventually enrolled in a native speaker Japanese-language course at her local community college and made several visits to Japan during her summer vacations, both of which improved her speaking ability and her literacy in the language. This led to an even closer connection with her bilingual friends, who now saw her as a full-fledged member of the social group.

In Meg's case, we can see that language exposure can affect group membership and group membership may in turn affect the amount of language exposure a learner receives. Considering this, heritage language programs are likely to be more successful if they provide language- and literacy-rich environments and promote group membership with speakers of the new language. Although research on heritage language education is scant, the studies available give some important clues about how best to promote both of these aims.

PROVIDING LANGUAGE EXPOSURE IN
HERITAGE LANGUAGE PROGRAMS

Drawing from what we know about effective language learning in general, and the available research on heritage language learning in particular, good language programs should do at least the following:

- Provide considerable exposure to the heritage language in oral and written forms.
- Create comfortable and nonthreatening learning environments where students are given opportunities and support to use the language, but are not required to do so until ready.
- Expose students to the types of language and language situations students themselves consider useful and important.
- Avoid overemphasis on teaching discrete language points or on the correctness of student speech or writing.
- Accept nonstandard forms of the language and value the varieties students speak.

Studies on classroom learning show that students learn most effectively and efficiently in classrooms containing these components, and language students themselves have identified these elements as conducive to their own language learning.[11]

Encourage Recreational Reading

Despite the relatively little research on heritage language development, some specific methods have emerged in recent years with promising and even impressive results. One of these is the promotion of recreational reading. Studies on recreational reading and language learning show that this method is highly successful in helping students become better readers, writers, and even speakers of the language. In school, recreational reading can be encouraged by giving students access to interesting and relevant books, liberty to choose which they read, time to read, and freedom to enjoy them without the encumbrance of tests or book reports. Used increasingly in the United States and other countries, recreational reading in the classroom has produced consistently better than or at least equivalent results to traditional skills and grammar-based methods for elementary, secondary, and adult students studying a second or foreign language.[12] But how do we know that this approach is beneficial for heritage language learners?

In 1998, Jeff McQuillan conducted a review of heritage language studies involving Spanish bilingual students in which he compared the outcomes of reading-based programs with programs that stressed grammar and vocabulary study. He included in his analysis programs that promoted reading through sustained silent reading (self-selected reading with no accountability required), literature or extensive reading programs (teacher-selected reading with some accountability required), and self-selected reading (students select their own reading again with some accountability). McQuillan grouped these programs together for the purposes of analysis because he believed that all three reading methods could provide highly engaging and comprehensible reading as long as teacher selections matched student interests and student accountability is kept to a minimum.

The studies included elementary-, secondary-, and university-level students and measured outcomes in reading ability, vocabulary knowledge, grammatical accuracy, amount of voluntary reading done, and student attitudes. As seen in the seven studies McQuillan reviewed, students who participated in the reading programs outperformed or did as well as those in traditional classrooms, with no cases of the traditional methods group outscoring the reading group.[13] These results are consistent with those of other research on pleasure reading conducted in the United States and in other countries, including research on students learning their first language, a second language, or a foreign language.[14]

Provide Appealing Reading Materials

A real obstacle exists, however, to promoting recreational reading among heritage language learners in the United States. Although we want students to read in school, the ultimate goal is to get students hooked on recreational reading so that they will read on their own and continue to get exposure to the language outside of school. But this is difficult to achieve because there is *little for students to read.*

In the United States, there is a documented dearth of reading materials in non-English languages, whether you look at school and classroom libraries, in bookstores and public libraries, or in students' homes.[15] If schools and communities want to help heritage language speakers become readers and writers, there are some easy first steps to take: Put more books in classroom and school libraries, and stock neighborhood libraries with a variety of reading materials at a wide range of proficiency levels. Then, give students easy and frequent access to them by taking regular class trips and informing parents of their availability. Giving students access to materials they are likely to read, such as comic books, teen novels, and magazines, at school and in the community is a necessary first step in fostering an interest in reading in the heritage language.

PROMOTING GROUP MEMBERSHIP IN
HERITAGE LANGUAGE PROGRAMS

In addition to giving learners as much exposure to the heritage language as possible, we also want to promote group membership by cultivating positive opinions about the language and its speakers. What does the research tell us about the types of programs likely to do this?[16]

As I mentioned earlier, remarkably little research has been done on heritage language programs in the United States, in part because so few publicly supported programs exist. We can, however, look for evidence from other countries where programs have been established to promote minority languages. North and South American studies have produced research results and program descriptions that allow us to draw some tentative conclusions about what may be useful in the United States.

In general, programs promote positive group membership when they

- give official sanction and status to the heritage language by integrating it into the regular school-day curriculum, rather than relegating it to an after-school or weekend program;
- incorporate enjoyable and interesting exposure to the language in school and give students opportunities to interact using the language; and
- cultivate interest in and appreciation of other languages and cultures among both minority and *majority* language speakers.

A program documented by Grace Feuerverger of the University of Toronto, for example, shows how even a small intervention containing these elements in one culturally diverse elementary school can have dramatic effects on students' language and heritage group attitudes, as well as on the students' own self-esteem. At the school Feuerverger studied, the librarian added to the library holdings non-English-language books reflecting the linguistic diversity in the school and encouraged teachers to use the books in their own classrooms. Some teachers included the books in their content lessons as well as encouraged students to read and translate poems and stories for their classmates and to teach one another words and phrases in their heritage language. One teacher commented that the books not only were used by the minority language speakers, but also benefited the monolingual English speakers. She observed: "Monolingual children react much more positively. It's a whole world they didn't know about."[17] In one case, after a Chinese-speaking girl finished telling a story, an Iranian boy said that he wished that he could read Chinese. Feuerverger observed that students learned to appreciate and respect those who come from backgrounds other than their own and who spoke languages other than English.

Students themselves gained confidence as they were given opportunities to interact with their fellow students through books. Feuerverger interviewed Alex, an 8-year-old boy from Bulgaria who had just finished reading and translating a story for his third-grade class, and she could see that his "confidence was glowing as he translated the story for me into English."[18] This program not only promoted heritage language development, but also brought about school validation of the students' linguistic and cultural backgrounds.[19]

School Support

The role that the heritage language plays in a school's curriculum can have substantial influence on the attitudes students develop toward that language. In the literacy intervention documented by Feuerverger that I just described, the school signaled the books' importance by focusing both student and teacher attention on their presence and by promoting their use. In another study by Feuerverger, we can again see how giving official sanction to the heritage language can have dramatic effects on student opinions.[20] In this study, the attitudes of Italian-Canadian eighth-graders in two Toronto schools were compared. In one school, students participated in an Italian heritage language program integrated within the regular school day. In the other, students had the option to enroll in Italian classes offered on Saturday mornings, separate from their regular classes during the week. Feuerverger found significant differences between the schools with and without integrated programs in terms of how students rated the language's status and the students' own language ability. Students in the integrated program had positive attitudes toward Italian and high levels of confidence in using the language as compared to the other group. In contrast, Feuerverger found strong feelings among the students in the after-school program that Italian was not a legitimate school subject. Also very telling is the low degree of willingness to participate in the study itself: Only 1 student out of the 67 potential subjects from the integrated day program group chose not to participate, whereas 23 out of 67 possible subjects from the Saturday program declined to participate. It is likely that the lower degree of priority given the language and the lack of legitimacy it held because it was not a regular school subject resulted in students in the Saturday program getting less exposure to the language and developing significantly lower opinions of it. This and other studies suggest that successful heritage language programs need to be incorporated into the overall school curriculum in order to elevate its status in the eyes of the students.

Another international study, this one conducted in Peru, also found that school support is important and can have significant impact on students' self-esteem and performance in school. Researcher Nancy Hornberger investigated attitudes and behaviors of Quechua-speaking elementary students in a school with heritage language support (a maintenance bilingual education Quechua-Spanish program) and those enrolled in a Spanish-only school. She made observations and tape recordings of class sessions and found that the minority children in the Spanish-only (majority language) school suffered far more stress than those in the bilingual education program. She observed that the students in the Spanish-only school with no heritage language support refused to participate or misbehaved substantially more than the students in the maintenance bilingual education program. Hornberger concluded:

> My impression was that much of their misbehaviour stemmed from the stress of being in an environment which they did not understand, the more so because so much happened in a language not entirely familiar to them. It appeared to me that they were used to being in control of a situation and felt very much left out of control in the classroom.[21]

In response to their misbehavior, teachers punished the children, who "often did not understand what was required of them . . . in contrast, I did not observe corporal punishment in the bilingual classrooms." Considering these conditions, it would be reasonable to predict that these students would want to acquire Spanish as quickly as possible and perhaps distance themselves from the language of the home, and will experience ethnic evasion (see Chapter 3).

School support may be so vital that without it, the task of promoting the heritage language is severely handicapped. As part of her master's thesis at California State University, Long Beach, Kathy Brook conducted a study of after-school heritage language programs supported by the community or church that enrolled Japanese American second- and third-generation students. She found through surveys and interviews that students didn't enjoy their extra time at the school and that they attended grudgingly:

> Most Japanese American children resent having to attend Japanese schools on Saturdays while their non-Japanese counterparts are free to use that time as they please. Other commitments—such as public school homework, participation in sport leagues, taking piano lessons or dance classes—often seem more important to the children. According to one consultant [survey respondent], even though many *Sansei* [third-generation Japanese Americans] have gone to Japanese language schools, they tend to see it as a punishment—"a terrible thing they had to do as a kid."[22]

Interesting Activities and Reading Materials

She suggests that another factor contributing to these students' ill feelings were the teaching methods used, which "may not be conducive to second language learning," a sentiment reflected in the comments of heritage language school graduates in the study. One graduate of the school said that there "was nothing inspirational about spending weekends in a spartan language classroom where the emphasis was on memorization," while others described studying grammatical rules and doing other form-focused tasks as tedious. These grammar and skills-based classes tended to provide very little exposure to meaningful and interesting language. The program Brook described violated at least two out of the three suggestions for cultivating group membership: The program was "add on" and did not validate the importance of the language in the eyes of the students, and it did not provide interesting and meaningful exposure to the language.

Expanding Our Notion of Group Membership

If group membership is important for heritage language development, then, which group memberships are required? While membership with the "native speaker" group(s) is certainly one possible option for encouraging language learning, it is by no means the only option. As long as the group we join considers language to be an important part of group membership, then the effects are similar.

My own case illustrates this point. When I began to develop my heritage language in college, I studied abroad in Taiwan for several months at a Mandarin language center at a Taiwanese university. (My heritage language is actually Cantonese Chinese but my university only offered Mandarin Chinese.) While I was in Taipei, the group I aspired to join was not one consisting of local residents, but rather, another group of Mandarin speakers: other international students studying at the same Chinese university who were in the language levels above mine. I didn't see myself as a future Taiwanese citizen. Instead, I wanted to be an English-language speaker who was highly proficient in Mandarin. I socialized with the members of the group and felt that I gained some level of acceptance as a result of my growing competence in the language. And as my Mandarin improved, so too did my status in the group. Even though Mandarin was not generally the language of communication among the group members, when in the community, the most Mandarin-proficient members spoke for the rest of the group in such things as ordering food in restaurants and asking for information. This of course had the predictable effect. I wanted to continue improving my Mandarin and did so over those months. As long as language is an important component of group membership, then our attitudes toward and interest in the language are likely to be affected.

For this reason, in terms of our heritage language students, it is not essential that they identify with native-speaker peers in other countries where the language is spoken. As long as they are able to feel allegiance with a group that deems the language important—such as bilingual and biliterate students in their school—then the positive effects are similar.

Having made a case for developing heritage languages, in this chapter I discussed what can be done to establish effective educational programs. I summarized what the second-language-acquisition field identifies as two of the major factors contributing to language development, language exposure and group membership, focusing on how they are relevant to heritage languages. Studies available on heritage language programs and their effects on student outcomes, both language development and attitudes, suggest that these two factors are indeed important for heritage language programs if they are to foster positive language attitudes and promote high levels of language proficiency.

CHAPTER 6

Where Do We Go From Here?

In the early 1990s, I saw a British film about a young boy who was slowly losing his sight. As the boy's vision grew progressively worse, he exchanged one pair of glasses for another, always heavier and thicker than the previous pair. One day, he attended a family gathering and as he sat on a stoop across the street observing his relatives assembling for picture taking, he took off his glasses, something he seldom did during daylight hours. As he looked around without his customary specs, he saw to his surprise that everyone else was blind, wearing dark glasses and carrying canes; he was the only one who could see.

This strange and haunting scene is analogous to today's public perception of the language situation in the United States. The true circumstances have been obscured by thick lenses that, when removed, reveal a picture very much the opposite of the illusion they had created. The thick glasses through which we've observed language issues have become thicker and thicker as misinformation heaps upon misunderstanding to create a badly warped image of how immigrants and their children fare in their new country. In this book, I have attempted to remove these obscuring lenses to reveal a more accurate view of language learning in the United States.

WHAT IS THE CURRENT SITUATION?

One of the greatest challenges to improving English-language education and fostering bilingualism in the United States is public opinion in two major areas: immigrant language learning and the role of heritage languages. First, misinterpretation of immigrants' level of desire to learn English has led many to perceive non-English-language communities and the availability of services in other languages as indications of structural resistance to English. However, a closer look reveals that communities and services in immigrant languages give newcomers access to the very resources—such as employment and ESL classes—that ease their integration into U.S. society and promote their English-language learning long term.

Another related belief is that new arrivals resist using English, which in turn hampers their English-language development. Upon reflection, it seems natural for new arrivals to continue using in the home and among friends and family the language they know best, and one they've used throughout most of their life. This continued use of the heritage language in no way mitigates the learning of English. As I discussed in chapters 3 and 4, immigrants are well aware that English fluency is a prerequisite to gaining access to the resources available in the United States. Knowing this, immigrants generally add English as a second language to their first, an effective strategy that allows them to communicate and have full participation in both personal and public sectors.

The failure to understand that adding a new language to an existing one is both possible and desirable has also led to a second set of misconceptions among the public. Because many believe in the myth that simultaneous development of two languages will result in inferior learning of both, the proposed solution is for students to forget or at least put aside their heritage language while they learn English. The contrary is true, as I discussed in Chapter 3. The minority language plays an important and useful role in reaching two critical goals: the learning of English and the learning of school subjects. Moreover, if the heritage language is supported, students can become bilingual and biliterate, which allows them to garner the demonstrated cognitive, academic, and career advantages for their own advancement and to make economic, political, and educational contributions to society. The public has yet to recognize these multiple advantages to fostering heritage language development.

To summarize, in the preceding chapters, I have argued the following:

- The idea that immigrants and their children don't learn English and resist doing so is a prominent argument used to support language restriction policies (Chapter 1).
- This belief is in fact based upon a myth. Abundant evidence shows that both adult immigrants and their children are, by and large, learning English well and at a rapid pace, despite limited personal resources and opportunities to learn (Chapter 2).
- Children of immigrants, in fact, favor English over their heritage language, which has spelled the systematic loss and eventual death of the heritage language in immigrant families (Chapter 3).

- The true language crisis, then, is loss of heritage languages, curtailing opportunities to become bilingual and to reap the important benefits, both personal and societal, of dual-language proficiency (Chapter 4).
- By devoting attention and resources to heritage language development (Chapter 4), and implementing programs that are consistent with effective and promising language learning methods, it may be possible to mitigate, to some extent, the loss of these valuable languages for the good of immigrant families and for society at large (Chapter 5).

WHERE DO WE GO FROM HERE?

Myths about immigrant language learning skew the public mindset on language-related issues, causing a misdirection of energy and funds toward solving phantom problems while ignoring true crises. If public views on these issues can be shifted, English-language learning and bilingualism can be encouraged through measures such as those described below.

English-Language Learning

There are concrete steps that can be taken to improve English-language learning and to support heritage language development. Although the information discussed in this book shows an encouraging picture of how well immigrant adults and children are currently faring, it also points to obstacles that still remain. These obstacles, once removed, would likely increase the much needed opportunities for English-language learning both for adults and children.

First, for immigrant adults, we need to support widely and systematically implemented free or low-cost English-language-learning programs that take into account the often limited resources and sometimes unique work demands of immigrant learners. Currently, some adult education programs are available through selected public school districts that have recognized the need for ESL classes in their communities, but these offerings can be costly and are insufficient in number to meet the demand. Also costly are community college courses and private language schools, which are typically tuition driven. These primary sources of ESL instruction are woefully inadequate to serve the existing and growing population of immigrant adults.

Second, for the children of immigrants, support and funding is needed to reinforce and build bilingual education programs for English-language-learning youths. Bilingual education is the most soundly supported educational approach for ensuring that students learn English well while they also keep up with school subjects. At present, bilingual education is a highly controversial topic among politicians and the public at large, the controversy fueled by media coverage of disgruntled parents or teachers or misinterpreted student outcomes. Bilingual education programs, like other educational programs, are not without room for improvement. However, they remain the best documented program to educate English-learning students. Rather than advocating for dismantling bilingual education because of its current shortcomings, some have argued that energy needs to be focused on remedying flaws, such as shortages of bilingual teachers and educational resources, which would make such programs even more effective. As these resources become available, the number of bilingual programs also need to be expanded to include more students who are currently in less effective types of programs or no special programs at all, including those who speak less common heritage languages. By providing adults and children with optimal programs in sufficient numbers, the current success of English-language learners can be bolstered and their numbers increased.

Heritage Language Development

In terms of heritage language development, we need to recognize heritage language education as a national priority and build public awareness and support for language preservation. Heritage language education is currently being supplied by the few high school or college foreign-language programs that have recognized the need, and community schools with no public financial support. What is needed are efforts to (1) help schools recognize heritage language education as being important, and (2) supply the necessary conditions for the development of the language.

The steps outlined below are based on the research currently available on second-language development in general, and heritage language education in particular. The latter is a field in need of far more attention, although the following components have proved useful in programs thus far or hold promise in light of past successes:

- Systematic heritage language programs beginning in kindergarten and through postsecondary education.
- Heritage language curriculum integrated into the regular school day for heritage language speakers. To prepare for an increasingly global community, non-heritage-language speakers in the same class or school will study foreign languages.

- The development of a corps of multilingual teachers with an awareness of heritage language issues, including an understanding of the language minority youth experience in the United States.
- Mass availability of appropriate educational resources in the heritage language—such as subject matter textbooks, computer programs, and recreational reading materials—that match student needs and interest.

These measures would serve as a foundation for establishing heritage language development as a legitimate and important education priority in the United States.

If we take away the obstructing specs, we see through the language fallacies in the United States and gain a clear view of the facts. By doing so, we can begin to shift from battling phantom resistance to learning English and advocating English monolingualism as a result, to promoting bilingualism and biliteracy (and multilingualism and multiliteracy) among immigrants and their children to counteract the very real forces of language shift. The strategies in this chapter serve as a starting point in affecting this fundamental and critical paradigmatic change.

Notes

Chapter 1

1. According to Crawford (1999a), the following states have adopted official English legislation: Alabama (1990), Alaska (1998), Arizona (1988), Arkansas (1987), California (1986), Colorado (1986), Florida (1988), Georgia (1996), Hawaii (1978), Illinois (1969), Indiana (1984), Kentucky (1984), Mississippi (1987), Missouri (1998), Montana (1995), Nebraska (1923), New Hampshire (1995), North Carolina (1987), North Dakota (1987), South Carolina (1987), South Dakota (1995), Tennessee (1984), Virginia (1981), and Wyoming (1996).

2. The text of Proposition 227, by Ron Unz and Gloria Matta Tuchman (1997), is available online at Jim Crawford's Web site (http://ourworld.compuserve.com/homepages/JWCRAWFORD/unztext.htm), where he also provides a detailed analysis.

3. Where did these beliefs originate? Many writers have pointed out that attitudes toward language policy often stem from adverse feelings toward the people who speak the language (August & García, 1988; Crawford, 1992; Cummins, 1989; Dicker, 1996; Ricento, 1998). Even a cursory look at restrictions placed on language use in the past 150 years among immigrants to the United States and Native Americans in this country reveal that hidden motives have indeed driven many proponents of English-only.

One example of ulterior motives driving language restrictionism is the case of Japanese-language schools in Hawaii. As restrictive measures continued to limit language choice across the U.S. mainland in the early part of the 20th century, similar actions were being taken in Hawaii, with its large Japanese-speaking population. By 1917, a majority of students of Japanese descent attended public schools during the day and Japanese-language schools after school or on weekends. In 1934, the territory had 181 documented supplemental private Japanese schools.

Beginning in 1919, legislation was passed to restrict these schools, including requiring teachers to be certified on the basis of whether they embodied "ideals of democracy and [had] knowledge of English," even though these instructors taught the Japanese language and most were recent arrivals from Japan (cited in Hawkins, 1995, p. 33). In 1920, antagonism toward these schools prompted the

Territorial Attorney General in Hawaii to propose the abolition of all foreign-language schools. In 1919, the annual governmental report stated,

> There can neither be national unity in ideals nor in purpose unless there is some common method of communication through which may be conveyed the thought of the nation. All Americans must be taught to read and write and think in one language; this is a primary condition to that growth which all nations expect of us and which we demand of ourselves. (Cited in Hawkins, 1995, p. 35)

These types of restrictions resulted from a number of causes having little to do with language, including (1) suspicion of the Japanese prompted by their military actions in China in the 1920s; (2) the *haole* (white) elite's resentment of the Japanese community's growing labor power, including their instrumental participation in several major plantation strikes; and (3) distrust of non-Christian religions, including Buddhism (some of the first Japanese schools were established by Buddhist temples). As a result, the Japanese schools were seen as congregational and organizational centers for un-American activity and a symbol of the growing economic and political power of the Japanese community.

The tide for non-English languages and language restrictionism began to turn—at least on the U.S. mainland—when the 1960s civil rights movement gained momentum, galvanizing both local and federal advocacy of minority rights. In 1968, the federal government, which now focused some attention on the past and present inequities suffered by various minority groups, passed the Bilingual Education Act. The result of the passage of this act, together with previous legislation (such as the Economic Opportunity Act of 1964 and the Elementary and Secondary Education Act of 1965), resulted in the needs of minority groups, especially the large populations of Mexican Americans and Puerto Ricans, gaining increased attention. Language, then, is often a tool or symbol of covert social, political, or economic battles, and a proxy for other agendas.

4. *Proposing an amendment to the Constitution of the United States with regard to the English language*, 98th Cong., 1st Sess. (September 21, 1983) (testimony of Senator Huddleston).

5. *Legislation designating English the official language of the United States*, 101st Cong., 1st Sess. (January, 19, 1989) (testimony of Senator Shumway).

6. *Statements on introduced bills and joint resolutions*, 100th Cong., 1st Sess. (January 6, 1987) (testimony of Senator Symms).

7. *Statements on introduced bills and joint resolutions*, 99th Cong., 1st Sess. (January 22, 1985) (testimony of Senator Symms).

8. U.S. English, a powerful Washington-based lobbying organization, uses a similar argument to advocate official-English legislation. Take, for example, an excerpt from one of their Web pages devoted to addressing frequently asked questions (http://www.us-english.org/faqs.htm):

Q: Is official English legislation anti-immigrant?
A: Official English legislation is actually pro-immigrant. It encourages immigrants to learn English so they can truly enjoy the economic opportunities

available to them in this country. A "linguistic welfare" system that accommodates immigrants in their native languages eliminates the incentive to learn English and restricts them to low-skill, low-paying jobs.

These arguments are quite reminiscent of conversations overheard between parents and their children. Restrictions on language use, the logic goes, is in the interest of those being restricted. This argument casts immigrants not only as children who need guidance, but also as *bad* children who are unable to regulate their own behavior without external constraints or intervention.

9. *Introduction of bills and joint resolutions*, 104th Cong., 1st Sess. (January, 9, 1995) (testimony of Senator Selby).

10. *Statements on introduced bills and joint resolution*, 103rd Cong., 1st Sess. (February 24, 1993) (testimony of Senator Shelby).

11. In this study (McQuillan & Tse, 1996), we examined whether research on bilingual education had any impact on public opinion as reflected in letters to the editor and editorials in major newspaper and news magazines. In short, we discovered no relationship between the majority of the published research studies or meta-analyses that showed the superiority of bilingual education over other teaching methods, and the largely negative opinions expressed in the news sources about bilingual education.

12. Lamm, 1986, p. A23.

13. Evans, 1986, p. 76.

14. *New York Times*, September 27, 1985, p. A30.

15. Will, 1985, p. 78.

16. Yardley, 1994, p. B1.

17. Acle, 1991, p. M7.

18. Porter, 1990, p. B3.

19. Yardley, 1994, B1.

20. Language learning is a political issue, especially in the form of bilingual education. Bilingual education grew out of the civil rights struggles for equity to give students from minority backgrounds access to education. Although now considered by a majority of the research community to be theoretically and empirically sound, it has been under fire from "English only" groups who claim that bilingual education doesn't work and should be abandoned.

Why the continued attacks? Sonia Nieto (1996) has suggested that bilingual education remains a political issue because it has the potential to empower traditionally powerless and subordinate groups. The fear among the critics, she contends, is that bilingual education may produce these emancipatory changes and challenge the conventional wisdom that the native language and culture need to be burdened and forgotten for students to succeed and to become "real Americans" (p. 195).

Therefore, bilingual education is not only beneficial for learning English, but may have far-reaching effects in equalizing power disparities in the United States. Jim Cummins (1989) warned, however, that bilingual education in and of itself will not have these desired effects unless teachers and schools attempt to reverse the institutionalized racism endemic among society at large. Unless school programs actively promote an antiracist agenda, bilingual education programs may inadvertently perpetuate the very discriminatory structures and practices they seek to eliminate.

21. Unz, 1997, p. M6.

22. Pedroza, 1998, p. G3.

23. Smith, 1998, p. B7.

Chapter 2

1. According to the U.S. Census Bureau website (www.census.gov), the U.S. population in December 1999 was approximately 273 million.

2. Boswell, 1998. Chapter 4 in the present volume provides a more extensive discussion of the economic benefits of bilingualism for the individual as well as for U.S. economic competitiveness.

3. The data is from a report by the National Association of Latino Elected and Appointed Officials Education Fund and the Tomás Rivera Policy Institute (1998). The data were collected in Los Angeles (for Guatemalans and Salvadorans) and New York City (for Dominican and Colombians) in census tracts with 10% or more population density for at least one of the four groups. Thirty-minute telephone interviews were conducted with 1,503 respondents: Colombians (375), Dominicans (377), Guatemalans (376), and Salvadorans (375). The interviews were conducted in either Spanish or English according to the respondent's preference. Those who arrived between 1986 and 1997 included Colombians (41.9%), Dominicans (52.9%), Guatemalans (74.6%), and Salvadorans (78.2%); those over 18 at their age of immigration were Colombians (65.5%), Dominicans (64.5%), Guatemalans (66.6%), and Salvadorans (67.1%).

4. These immigrants give various reasons for coming to the U.S., chief among them joining family, economic reasons, or political strife.

	Colombian	Dominican	Guatemalan	Salvadoran
Join family	34.6%	33.8%	16.2%	16.7%
Flee political strife	.6%	1.5%	16.5%	25.0%
For job	7.6%	10.6%	7.1%	9.7%
Economic reasons	29.6%	37.1%	41.8%	34.4%

5. I am grateful to Lisa R. (personal communication, May 24, 2000) for allowing me to interview her for the purposes of this book.

6. Portes and Hao (1998) included in their sample those students with at least one parent born outside of the United States or who had been in the United States for at least 5 years at the time of the study.

7. See, for example, Kominski, 1989, cited in MacArthur, 1993.

8. Rong and Preissle (1998) used the census "mircodata," a special, detailed database consisting of the responses of a representative sample (5%) of the U.S. population. Their results are therefore reflective of the U.S. population as a whole.

9. Quintanilla, 1995, p. E7.

10. Portes and Rumbaut (1996) conducted the first study mentioned and Rumbaut (1995) carried out the other analysis.

11. Among low-income families, 12% of English-proficient foreign-born students ages 16 to 18 had dropped out of school, compared with 15% of English-only students. Among high-income students, 8.2% of fluent English-proficient foreign-born students were dropouts, compared with 8% of native-born youth.

12. Driscoll (1999) analyzed data from the National Education Longitudinal Study of 1988.

13. Grant and Rong (1999) examined the number of years of schooling completed by foreign-born immigrants, the children of immigrants (U.S. born but with at least one foreign-born parent), and native-born youths (U.S. born with both parents U.S. born), ages 15 to 24. Adjusting for the age of the youths, the study determined that the children of immigrants had slightly, more years of education completed than those who were U.S. native-born (11.7 versus 11.6 years). Foreign-born youths had somewhat lower number of years completed (10.8), although these figures do not take into account either the number of years students had been in the United States, nor their parent's level of education, both of which strongly affect drop-out rate. However, caution should be taken in interpreting these findings, since the sample of 15- to 24-year-olds may include those who never attended school in the United States, a major limitation to the study.

14. While many children of immigrants are doing well, some are still failing. How can the two primary goals—learning English and succeeding academically—be further promoted and supported? One such effort is a controversial but highly effective program aimed at helping children who enter school limited in English: bilingual education. Bilingual education has existed in the United States since the earliest days of the colonies. Historically, many immigrant communities have set up day schools to teach subjects in the native language. In fact, German-medium schools existed in fairly large numbers until the onset of World War I. (Crawford, 1999b). More recently, bilingual education programs have been used to teach Spanish, Chinese, Armenian, and many other language speakers across the United States.

The aims of bilingual programs are precisely those advocated for all immigrants. First, these programs make learning English a top priority and students receive English as a second language (ESL) instruction from the very beginning of the program. Second, students continue to learn school subjects—math, science, social studies, among others—in their native language while they learn the new language. This ensures that students don't fall behind their native-English-speaking peers in academic achievement and allows the English learners to join the all-English classes as soon as possible without remediation. This reduces the chances of students failing in school.

Bilingual education is actually one of the most well-researched educational approaches in the field of education, and studies are fairly consistent in their positive evaluation. A number of these studies have compared the performance of students enrolled in two types of programs—bilingual education and ESL-only—and have found that students in well-implemented bilingual education classes learned English more effectively and have higher academic achievement than students who don't get support for school subjects in the native language (Greene, 1997; Willig, 1985).

While research strongly supports bilingual education, only a small percentage of all limited English proficient students in the U.S. are in such programs. For instance, California, which has the largest English-learning student population in the United States, enrolled less than one third of eligible students in bilingual education during the 1994–95 school year (California Department of Education, 1995). The rest of the students were placed in classes taught only in English with some instructional modifications or in regular mainstream classes with little or no special support. One reason for so few eligible students enrolled in bilingual education programs is a lack of bilingual teachers (Olsen, 1997), and the situation is likely to be exacerbated by a political movement begun in the late 1990s to outlaw bilingual education. In California, a law was passed in 1998 that banned bilingual education in public schools, and similar measures have been proposed in other states.

15. See, for example, Espenshade & Fu (1997) and McManus, Gould, & Welch (1983).

16. See Krashen (1996) for his discussion.

An obvious problem with making sweeping claims about differences between cultural groups is the diversity found within each of those groups. For example, the term *Asian* encompasses East Asians, who include those from Korea, Japan, and China; Southeast Asians, from Vietnam, Laos, and Cambodia; and South Asians, from India and Pakistan. Also often included under the term Asian are Pacific Islanders, from such regions as Hawaii and Samoa.

Even within an ethnic group, Wong and López (2000) point out, there may be significant socioeconomic and cultural differences. Take, for example, the case of Chinese immigrants to the United States. One group of Chinese arrivals are Hong Kong "wealthy investors who tried to protect themselves from uncertainty over Hong Kong's political future by emigrating and bringing capital to the United States before 1997," and other Chinese arrivals may be "sino-Vietnamese immigrants who may be successful entrepreneurs or welfare-dependent refugees" (p. 271).

The myth of the Asian "model minority" has been refuted on this and other grounds, with evidence showing drastically different achievement among these disparate group. Zhou (1999), for instance, analyzed 1990 Census data for six Asian American groups and found that among first-generation 16- and 17-year-olds, Vietnamese speakers had more than two to three times the drop-out rate (10.3%) compared with that of the Chinese (4.5%) and Japanese (3.8%) youth in the sample.

17. Among the other factors found to be important for literacy development is the availability of and close association with a peer group that uses the minority language and values it for group membership (Tse, in press).

18. Studies on language brokering include Malakoff & Hakuta (1991), a study that examined the accuracy of Spanish-English child bilingual translations; McQuillan & Tse's (1995) interview study of adult bilinguals reporting retrospec-

tively about their past brokering experiences; Orellana, Lam, & Meza (2000), an ethnography of adolescent girls who acted as primary brokers in their families; and Tse (1995 & 1996), two studies that surveyed high school Spanish-, Vietnamese-, and Chinese-speaking students on a variety of broker-related issues.

19. Orellana, Lam, and Meza (2000) provided examples of how language brokering may be a gender-delineated activity as well, with the girls in the families she studied expected to remain at home or to accompany their parents to serve as brokers, while the boys were not expected to take on these responsibilities.

20. In a survey of 64 students speaking Chinese, Vietnamese, or both, all but 5 indicated that they had brokered (Tse, 1995), and in a survey of Spanish-speaking students, all 35 reported having brokered at one time or another (Tse, 1996).

21. In this study, the interview respondents indicated that language brokering of the type Anita engaged in had positive effects on their oral language and literacy development in both languages. A majority of those U.S. born noted how brokering helped them improve their heritage language ability, while those born abroad indicated that brokering spurred their English-language learning (McQuillan & Tse, 1995).

22. See Wagner & Venezky (1999) for a discussion of the current state of adult literacy in the United States.

23. U.S. Bureau of Census (1997), *Profile of the Foreign-Born Population in the United States*, Table 10–1B, http://www.census.gov/population/www/socdemo/foreign/foreign98.html

24. U.S. Department of Education, 1998. The data is derived from the 1995 National Household Education Survey, which used a random-digit-dial telephone survey to obtain a nationally representative sample of the 50 states and the District of Columbia. The survey was conducted in January to April 1995 and included adults age 16 or older who were not enrolled in elementary or secondary school at the time of the interview.

25. See López (2000) for a brief description and additional references on the Central Intelligence Agency and Hmong political alliance in Laos and the circumstances that eventually lead to the U.S. resettlement.

26. Weinstein-Shr (1994) conducted an ethnography among the Hmong refugee community in Philadelphia and focused on the uses of literacy among several of her ESL students. The descriptions of Chou Chang are drawn from her study.

27. Weinstein-Shr, 1994, p. 54.

28. Weinstein-Shr, 1994, p. 54.

29. Again, only estimates are available on the number of adults requiring ESL services (Friedenberg, 1995; U.S. Department of Education, 1998).

30. Beason, 1997, B3.

31. Migrant Health Program, 1990, as cited in Bartlett & Vargas, 1991.

32. Kissam & Griffith, 1990, as cited in Velázquez, 1994–1995.

33. These profiles are taken from a press article by Arana-Ward (1997).

34. As Norton (2000a) points out, it is difficult to understand why languages are and are not learned without recognizing the underlying power relationships between majority and minority language speakers and how those relationships shape identity. (Norton provides a concise and useful definition of identity: "I use

the term identity to reference how a person understand his or her relationship to the world, how that relationship is constructed across time and space and how the person understands possibilities for the future" [p. 5].)

She argues that

> the concept of *investment* rather than *motivation* more accurately signals the socially and historically constructed relationship of learners to the target language, and their sometimes ambivalent desire to learn and practice it. The notion is best understood with reference to the economic metaphors that Bourdieu uses in his work—in particular the notion of *cultural capital* . . . I take the position that if learners invest in a second language, they do so with the understanding that they will acquire a wider range of symbolic and materials resources, which will in turn increase the value of their cultural capital. . . . Thus the notion presupposes that when language learners speak, not only are they exchanging information with target language speakers, but they are constantly organizing and reorganizing a sense of who they are and how they relate to the social world. (p. 444)

Identity, then, is important because it determines in large part how we think about the languages around us, and ultimately, determine such things as our level of interest in learning languages, and how, when, and with whom we use them.

Chapter 3

1. The terms *language loss* and *language shift* have been used in the second-language-acquisition and bilingualism literature to refer to distinct and separate concepts, while at other times, interchangeably for the same phenomenon. In this book, I will use these terms to distinguish between language proficiency and language preference and use, and between intergenerational and intragenerational language changes. *Language loss* applies to intergenerational disappearance of the heritage language where each successive generation develops increasingly lower proficiency in the language. *Language shift* refers to changes in preferences and use of the heritage language in favor of English, either individually or within a group, over the course of one generation.

2. Josua Fishman (1966) documented a three-generation process for "language shift" among immigrants families. Research by a number of other scholars has confirmed this general pattern among immigrant communities in the United States and in other countries (see, for example, Hornberger, 1998; Veltman, 1983; Wong Fillmore, 1991).

3. Portes & Hao (1998) is one of the few recent large-scale studies of language shift and loss across language groups. Also see Chapter 2 in the present book for further discussion of this study's results on English-language learning.

4. See, for example, Cummins (1993), Pease-Alvarez & Winsler (1994), and Wong Fillmore (1991), who have documented cases of preschool and elementary students stopping the development of the heritage language or shifting in their language use and preferences to English or both.

5. I am grateful to Rick (personal communication, January 22, 2000) for allowing me to recount his language history for the purposes of this book.

6. See Hernandez-Chavez (1993), who argues that language shift may not always follow a generational pattern, and may be determined instead by the social and linguistic contact between families and communities.

7. Lambert (1974) used the term "subtractive bilingualism" to denote the learning of a second language while losing or halting the development of the first language, and "additive bilingualism" as the learning of a second language while maintaining or developing the first.

8. This *Hispanic Business* article (Reveron, 1998) is confirmed by other studies on the economic impact of bilingualism. See Chapter 4 in the present book for a more thorough discussion.

9. According to Wiley (1996, p. 19), the National Chicano Survey "was a bilingual survey of a nationally selected and representative sample of the Mexican-origin population in the United States." It was conducted by the Institute for Social Research, with financial support from the Ford Foundation and National Institutes of Health.

10. Social psychologists point out the importance of language as a symbol of group membership and its role in facilitating or limiting acceptance (Giles & Byrne, 1982).

11. Lee, 1991, p. 52.

12. Lee, 1979, p. 30.

13. I describe cases of ethnic evasion in two articles (1998a & 1998b); others have also documented this stage of adverse feelings toward the minority cultural group (see Phinney, 1991, for a review), although these earlier studies did not specifically address the role of language or how language is affected by identity formation.

14. See, for example, Schecter & Bayley (1997); Winsler, Diaz, Espinosa, & Rodriguez (1999); and Mitchell, Destino, & Karam (1998).

15. For descriptions of bilingual education programs, see, for example, Brisk (1998) and Faltis & Hudelson (1998).

16. Several of Kondo's (1998) second-generation Japanese American participants described the Japanese-language schools they attended as being more like child-care services and latchkey programs than traditional schools.

17. Brook (1988) and Kondo (1998) described Japanese-language schools, and Tse (in press) documented student experiences with both Japanese- and Chinese-language programs.

18. In an annual report on the number of limited English proficient students in the United States and the educational services available to them by state, Macías (1998) noted the small number of federally funded (Title VII) maintenance bilingual education programs for 1994–1997.

19. Valdés (1997) mentions a figure of 22% of all U.S. colleges and universities as offering special programs for heritage language Spanish speakers (Teschner, personal communication, March 4, 1994, as cited in Valdés, 1997), although she does not specify how this figure was derived.

20. Kondo (1998) concluded in her study of second-generation Japanese

American college students that the influence of Japanese mothers in providing exposure to the language in and out of the home was a major contributor to heritage language maintenance.

21. Lee, 1991, p. 35.

22. Lee, 1991, p. 47.

23. Schecter and Bayley (1997) conducted ethnographic interviews with families who immigrated to the United States from South America from different socioeconomic backgrounds.

24. Both quotes in this paragraph are from Soto (1997), p. 32.

25. Julie is one of ten interview participants in a larger study on heritage language maintenance and development (Tse, in press).

26. Lopez (1996) shows that linguistically concentrated communities in Los Angeles, for example, are generally populated by recent immigrants speaking their mother tongue, and provides data on intergenerational language loss among both Spanish-speaking and Asian-language-speaking groups. He points out that Spanish appears to be more resilient than Asian languages with fewer second-generation immigrants using primarily English in the home, which, he contends, is largely due to the number of speakers and their concentration in the United States, and the institutional supports that emerge to bolster the language. Lopez notes that while Spanish seems to linger longer over generations than some other non-English languages, the second generation is clearly learning English, a point supported by Portes and Hao (1998) (see Chapter 2 in the present book for a discussion).

27. Hagan (1994) conducted an ethnographic study of the Maya community from Guatemala living in Houston and documented the pattern of settlement in the United States based on personal networks and described it this way:

The pioneer migrant, for whatever idiosyncratic reason, chooses a place to settle. . . . The pioneer then brings over those closest to him from the home community. . . . This is the initial network in the migrant community. Once established in the host community, each person in this embryonic network reaches out to others in the home community, who then becomes potential migrants. . . . In the home and community, word spreads concerning the success of these early and adventurous pioneers; the motivation to migrate builds. . . . Over time, the migrant community grows in size as these networks reach out from the immediate family to incorporate other kin and eventually anyone from the home community. Over a period of years, even neighboring communities are networked in to the migration process. . . . The networks grow in strength and resiliency as the migrants adapt to the new conditions and demands of the host society (Massey et al., 1987). Thus, the neighborhood networks, housing networks, and job networks develop. With the establishment of these now multiple, overlapping networks, the cost of migration for the newcomer . . . are reduced as they increasingly arrive in the new community with access to a rich array of social resources. These include initial housing, job referrals, and information about how to get along in the host society. (pp. 152–154)

28. Veltman (2000) points out, on the basis of language-shift data, that language maintenance alone "cannot account for the increased presence of Spanish; most of this presence is explained by a large, continuous stream of new Spanish-speaking immigrants to the United States" (p. 62).

29. See Santa Ana (1993) and Zentella (1982) for discussions of Chicano English and examples of its distinctiveness from standard English; and Downing, Truitner, & Truitner (1980) for a rare description of Vietnamese English spoken among English speakers in Vietnam and immigrants to the United States.

30. This incident was reported in a *New York Times* article (Clines, 2000); see Wolfram, Temple Adger, & Christian (1999) for a discussion of dialects of English in the United States and the biases faced by speakers of nonstandard varieties.

31. There are different types of codeswitching, which can take place within a conversation, switching at the clause or sentence boundary ("intersentential"), or within a sentence ("intrasentential") (Gumperz, 1982; Hoffman, 1991; Romaine, 1995). Bilinguals codeswitch for a number of reasons. Gumperz (1982) examined language choice at the microlevel as a function of social interactions, and identified six major social purposes for conversational codeswitching, including the use of quotations, making interjections, establishing qualifications, reiterating, and personifying or objectifying. Codeswitching is also done in many situations to underscore an individual's personal involvement and their desire to be understood (Hoffman, 1991). Establishing group identity with a bilingual community is another major social purpose for codeswitching and has been documented in immigrant communities as well as among majority-language speakers in order to be accepted by a particular group (Calsamiglia & Tusón, 1984; Hewitt, 1982). Choices are made regarding which language to use in codeswitching, Myers-Scotton (1993) contends, according to an individual's judgment about which set of rights and obligations are necessary to signal and establish particular social relationships. As MacSwan (1999) points out, however, the ability to make predictions about language choice based on such data is extremely difficult considering the complexity of human interaction.

32. Schecter & Bayley, 1997, p. 524.

33. In another example of codeswitching, Bob and Albert, who work together in a brewery in Montreal and are bilingual in French and English, had this joking exchange:

Albert: Uh, it's like passing the buck to somebody but, uh, [laughs] can you spend some time with Perre Monday? It could be a good thing.

Bob: avec plaisir [with pleasure] . . . okay I'll do that. Uh, I charge Anne *rien* [nothing] but *spécial pour toi* [especially for you] 45 dollars an hour. [Translations added. Holler, 1992, p. 134.]

34. Timm (1993) gives a general overview of codeswitching and provides a number of excellent examples of both intersentential and intrasentential codeswitching in historical and present-day contexts.

35. Valdés, 2000, p. 113.

36. Alejandra Sotomayor (personal communication, September 14, 1999). An excerpt from the transcript of the August 17, 1999 *Don and Mike Show* broadcast from Albuquerque, New Mexico, on KHTL 920 AM was posted on the "AZBLE: Forum for Discussion of Bilingual Education in Arizona" listserv.

Chapter 4

1. Throughout this and other chapters, I discuss language proficiency issues for both English and heritage languages. It is important to point out that I am referring to oral language and literacy ability as two separate types of language knowledge that involve some distinct sets of skills and are not hierarchical in importance. That is, literacy is not a superior or more advanced form of language expression than oral proficiency.

2. Krashen (1996) reviewed the available research on literacy transfer across languages with different orthographies, concluding that even when the writing systems are different (1) "the underlying process of reading in different languages is similar," and (2) "the process of the development of literacy is similar in different languages" (p. 23). Krashen comes to these conclusions on the basis of studies on miscue analysis, reading score predictors, eye-fixation, and reading strategies, involving languages using the Roman alphabet and other orthographies, including Yiddish, Chinese, Japanese, Arabic, Hebrew, Burmese, Urdu, Navaho, Yoruba, Vietnamese, Turkish, and Dutch.

3. The cases of Mikhail and Andrei are used here for illustration only. Although I describe Andrei as immigrating from a small farming village in Russia, a majority of the 454,000 former Soviet Union immigrants residing in the United States as of 1995 are from large urban areas (Hinkel, 2000).

4. This is, in fact, what bilingual education programs do. See Chapter 3 for a description.

5. The two analyses on academic achievement and aspirations were conducted by Neilsen and colleagues (Fernandez & Nielsen, 1986, and Nielsen & Lerner, 1986, respectively). Peal and Lambert (1962) carried out the seminal study on balanced bilinguals, refuting previous claims that bilingualism carried negative cognitive effects. Peal and Lambert pointed out that those earlier studies did not control for level of English ability so that nonfluent English speakers were included in the samples. This, according to the researchers, was a critical flaw. Others have confirmed Peal and Lambert's findings that bilinguals have cognitive and problem-solving advantages over monolinguals (see, for example, Bialystock, 1987).

6. Moll (1992) and others (e.g., Zhou & Bankston, 1994) have called attention to the sources of knowledge often available through family and community members, resources often not recognized or valued by mainstream schools. Not only do those without heritage language proficiency lack access to these valuable resources; others have documented the difficulties that result from the break in communication between immigrant generations when language loss and language shift occurs (Mouw & Xie, 1999; Wong Fillmore, 1991).

7. This study also found that Miami–Dade County Spanish-English bilinguals have the highest educational attainments, the lowest poverty rates, and the best-paying jobs (Boswell, 1998).

8. Crawford (1997, p. 13) noted:

Immigration is a major factor in the new diversity. The minority-language population grew by 38 percent during the 1980s; those who have difficulty with English, by 37 percent; and the number of foreign-born residents, by 40 percent. These statistics are causally related. Since 1965, federal immigration policy has increased both the volume and the diversity of newcomers, who now come largely from non-English-speaking countries (Vialet, 1991). The proportion of foreign-born nearly doubled, from 4.8 percent of the U.S. population in 1970 to 8.7 percent in 1994 (Census Bureau, 1995a).

9. Simon, 1980.

10. Clark, 2000, p. C1.

11. These figures are taken from an International Trade Administration Tourism Industries commissioned report (1998).

12. Reveron, 1998, p. 14.

13. This was reported in an article by Clark (2000). Interestingly, García and Otheguy (1994) found in their study of international companies that small and midsized businesses preferred employing bilingual managers and executives. Speaking the language of the client gave the company a competitive edge. In larger multinational corporations, however, top executives and managers can generally operate effectively without dual-language ability. These high-level executives are less likely to be sent abroad, relying instead on local representatives for the company.

14. See Clark, 2000, p. C1. García and Otheguy (1994) describe two studies conducted on the use of non-English languages at businesses operating in two ethnically mixed neighborhoods in New York City. In the largely Dominican neighborhood of Washington Heights, among the 136 businesses surveyed, 56% of the 540 employees were either Spanish-speaking monolinguals or Spanish-English bilinguals (Leon, Mendez, & Velazquez, 1993, as cited in Garía & Otheguy, 1994). The second study of Jackson Heights found that 77% of the 313 businesses surveyed conducted most of their business in a language other than English (Castillo et al., 1993, as cited in García & Otheguy, 1994).

15. Krashen (1998) reviewed two studies by Fishman (Fishman, 1990; Fishman, Cooper, & Rosenbaum, 1977) and concluded that "the better we know other languages, the better chance there is to sell to countries that use those languages. . . . Nurturing and developing heritage languages may be a good thing for the economy and the balance of trade" (p. 7).

16. The President's Commission on Foreign Language and International Studies, 1980, p. 12.

17. Defense Language Institute general information can be found at their Web site: http://www.monterey.org/langcap/dli.html.

18. The Stanford Working Group on Federal Programs for Limited-English-Proficient Students, 1993, p. 12, as cited in Cummins (1996), p. 221.

19. The President's Commission on Foreign Language and International Studies, 1980, p. 12

20. Draper (1989) noted that questionnaires were mailed to "the foreign language supervisor or other person responsible for FLs within the education agencies" of the 50 states and the District of Columbia, with an 84% response rate (p. 264).

21. Cho & Krashen, 1998, p. 34

22. Thomas and Cao (1999) presented several examples of interactions among members of a Sino-Vietnamese family who communicate using four languages: Vietnamese, Mandarin, Hainanese, and English. Their conversation excerpts demonstrate not only the linguistic but also the cultural gap between three generations living in the same household.

23. I documented the adverse reactions traditional foreign-language learners may have when placed in courses with heritage language speakers in Tse (2000b), and the disadvantages heritage language speakers feel when placed in classes with traditional foreign-language students in Tse (in press).

24. Ruíz (1984) proposed three "orientations" to viewing language planning: Language-as-problem, language-as-right, and language-as-resource. He pointed out that bilingual education critics and advocates have generally taken the first two views. He believes, however, that there are a number of benefits to taking the third view, that of bilingualism as a resource. Ruíz argues that this view holds promise for alleviating some of the conflicts that emerge as a result of seeing the language either as a problem or a right, namely that

> it can have a direct impact on enhancing the language status of subordinate languages; it can help to ease tensions between majority and minority communities; it can serve as more consistent way of viewing the role of non-English languages in U.S. society; and it highlights the importance of cooperative language planning. (pp. 25–26)

It should be noted that while these orientations are helpful in seeing the policy alternatives available, they are seldom the actual impetus for making language-related policies. Crawford (2000) notes that "orientations toward language *per se* are rarely determinants in policy decisions about language" because the interests of contending factions are never purely linguistic (p. 110).

25. Four underlying assumptions support this language-as-a-problem perspective. These four arguments have been used extensively in U.S. language debates to advocate for added restrictions on non-English languages, such as legislation to make English the official language of the United States (see Chapter 1). The first of these is the "tacit compact" argument, which holds that by being admitted into the new country, immigrants implicitly agree to wave any minority rights, including their rights to use the minority language. A second and related contention is the "take-and-give" argument, which claims that since immigrants are typically economically better off in the new country, they should give themselves up wholeheartedly to its language and culture, abandoning the old. Third, to ensure that future generations are not trapped in cultural ghettos and secluded from mainstream life, the "antighettoization" argument claims that immigrants should not pass on the language to their children. To do so is to create isolated linguistic pockets, dooming future generations to cultural and economic ostricization. Finally, the "national unity" argument holds that guarding against these cultural and linguistic ghettoes is necessary because non-English languages may easily become politically disrup-

tive and divisive forces. For the sake of national security, the host country has a right to demand language assimilation among immigrants (Kloss, 1971; Wiley & Lukes, 1996). These arguments have been rebutted by Crawford (1992) and others (Wiley & Lukes, 1996). As noted in Chapter 2 in the present book, however, the underlying assumptions that immigrants are not, in fact, learning English is itself false, undermining the whole notion of immigrant languages as a "problem."

26. Fixman (1990) interviewed 32 employees working in international operations of nine companies of varying types and sizes. These companies included four Fortune 500 industrial firms, a major accounting and consulting firm, a major bank, an import-export firm, and an office supplies manufacturer. She found that small companies trying to enter the global market were particularly aware of the value of foreign-language ability. Smaller corporations have less access to resources such as the hiring of foreign nationals as interpreters and translators, and they tend to deal in a worldwide network of smaller companies where English is less likely to be the lingua franca, findings consistent with García and Otheguy (1994).

García and Otheguy (1994) also examined the help-wanted section of the *New York Times* between 1970 and 1988, finding a range of jobs requiring proficiency in languages other than English. The large majority of these positions were clerical, with some of the advertisements for tourism agents, service workers, and business professionals. The top five non-English languages specified were Spanish, German, French, Japanese, and Italian, in that order.

27. Draper and Hicks (1996) noted that almost two thirds (64.5%) of all high school foreign-language study was in Spanish, followed by 22.3% in French.

28. Japanese: from 556 to 5,439; Chinese: from 1,085 to 2,708 (Padilla & Sung, 1997).

29. The President's Commission on Foreign Language and International Studies, 1980, p. 12. Both the report and Simon (1980) proposed far-reaching recommendations for restructuring and expanding foreign-language and international-study programs.

30. These figures provided by Starr (1994) are disheartening, but some foreign-language programs at both the high school and university levels are beginning to offer separate courses for heritage language speakers. This is necessary, Valdés (1992) argued, because of the starkly different language profiles and needs of the heritage language speaker as compared with the traditional foreign-language student. She contends that the typical program designed for foreign-language learners "is totally inappropriate for bilinguals" (p. 55), and advocates that foreign-language departments create a new division or branch focused on the language maintenance of immigrant students.

31. The latest school year for which figures are available is 1994–95:

	1991–92	1992–93	1993–94	1994–95
Developmental Bilingual Education	.3% (6,085)	.4% (8,587)	.3% (8,389)	.3% (9,855)

Chapter 5

1. This skit was performed as part of Gilda Radner's comedy special called *Gilda Live* (Nichols, 1980).

2. Krashen's (1985, 1993) reviews of second-language-acquisition studies suggest that learners who receive "comprehensible input" focused on meaning rather than form tend to acquire language more efficiently.

Researchers have disagreed with Krashen on other points, but generally concur that receiving input is crucial for language learning to occur. For example, Gass and Selinker's (1994) often cited "integrated" model includes as one of its central components the receiving and internalization of input.

3. There is abundant evidence that more exposure to literacy leads to higher literacy ability. Warrick Elley (1991, 1996), for example, has shown this to be true for English-language learners in a number of different countries, including Singapore, Sri Lanka, Fiji, New Zealand, and South Africa. In a series of studies published in the 1980s and 1990s, Elley and his colleagues implemented reading-focused English-as-a-foreign-language programs to gauge their effects on literacy development among elementary-school-age students versus traditional form- or grammar-focused curricula. In these studies involving more than 10,000 students, those receiving the literacy-rich intervention outperformed the traditional groups on a number of language measures, with the gap between the two groups widening the longer the program ran. Others have found similar results with students in the United States learning different languages, including English as a second language, at various age and ability levels.

4. Smith (1998) emphasizes the importance of joining the "literacy club" for those learning to read and write in a first language, and Giles and Byrne (1982) stress the importance of several components such as the level of "ethnolinguistic vitality" to encourage group membership.

5. For a discussion of social identity theory, see Tajfel & Turner (1979).

6. Language learning can be affected positively or negatively by judgments we make about the groups of speakers associated with the language. This notion of group membership is consistent with Gardner and Lambert's two types of motivation for learning a language. An "instrumental" orientation refers to "a desire to gain social recognition or economic advantages through knowledge of a foreign language," such as getting a job or getting into college (Gardner & Lambert, 1972, p. 14). An "integrative" orientation is a "desire to be like representative members of the other language community," such as a social clique in high school (p. 14). Whether you are integratively or instrumentally motivated affects language acquisition, these researchers argue, by determining to a large extent the amount of interaction you have with members of the target language community.

However, it is important to keep in mind Norton's (2000a) critique of Gardner and Lambert's emphasis on motivation as a primary predictor of language achievement. She points out that a learner's exposure to a language is not solely determined by his or her motives. Depending on the role each person plays in a particular situation and the power relationships between the agents, the learner may not be granted access to the types of interactions which provide exposure to language or be permitted to form group membership with members of the new speech community.

7. For general discussions of language and group membership, see Taylor, Bassili, & Aboud (1973) and Giles, Taylor, & Bourhis (1977). For a review of these issues as they relate to heritage language learning, see Tse (1998c).

8. Smith, 1998, p. 21.

9. Meg was one of ten biliterates interviewed as part of a study on heritage language literacy (Tse, 2000).

10. See Chapter 3 for a discussion of "language shift."

11. I conducted a study to examine university students' opinions about their foreign-language education. Fifty-one students wrote their language learning autobiographies, which I then analyzed qualitatively. The students' responses centered around three themes: (1) opinions about teacher interactions and methodology, (2) evaluation of their own level of success in foreign-language study, and (3) attribution for the proficiency they reached in the language (Tse, 2000).

12. Krashen (1993) refers to recreational reading as "free voluntary reading," and in his book, provides a review of first- and second-language method comparison studies on the effectiveness of this approach versus more traditional language arts and reading curricula.

13. McQuillan (1998b) noted an interesting pattern in the studies: Heritage language (HL) reading programs in the early elementary grades and at the university level tended to be successful, while programs aimed at junior and senior high school students produced equivocal results. The students, he suggested, may have been going through a period of ethnic ambivalence/evasion, where they felt little group membership with heritage language speakers. Without this group membership, even methods rich in language input can only affect modest effects.

There is evidence of this in the researchers' descriptions of what occurred in the classroom when heritage language books were introduced at the high school level. McQuillan points out that in both of Schön, Hopkins, and Vojir's studies (1984, 1985), the researchers noted stark differences between the reaction of the U.S.-born Mexican American students and those who were born in Mexico and immigrated. A teacher in the study reported that "Mexican-American students are embarrassed about these books in Spanish. They don't want to look at them— they stay far away from them," while the "minority who come from Mexico are interested in them" (p. 38). This is consistent with the stage of ethnic evasion where students want little to do with the heritage language as they attempt to distance themselves from what they see as the undesirable, low-status, and stigmatized heritage group.

14. In addition to Krashen's (1993) review, see also Elley (1991) and Pilgreen & Krashen (1993).

15. Studies have documented the lack of heritage language books even in close-knit heritage language–speaking communities, such as those found in southern California (Krashen, 1998; McQuillan, 1998a; Pucci, 1994; Pucci & Ulanoff, 1996).

16. I reviewed studies that looked at three indicators of group membership among HL students: (1) attitudes toward the HL, (2) attitudes toward the heritage

group, and (3) attitudes toward the learners themselves as a member of the heritage group (Tse, 1997). Of the 13 studies included in the review that looked at the first indicator—how participation in heritage language programs related to attitudes toward the heritage language itself—9 studies found favorable results among program participants when compared with nonprogram students, and 5 found no effects. When we look at attitudes toward the heritage group, our second category, those in HL programs had more positive attitudes in all the nine studies that contain data on this point. Finally, in terms of how students judged themselves as a member of the HL group, all five of the studies that examine this issue found that students felt better about themselves if they had or were currently participating in an HL programs. (See Tse, 1998b, for a summary of these studies.)

17. Feuerverger, 1994, p. 136.

18. Feuerverger, 1994, p. 137.

19. It is unclear whether any of the elementary students observed in the study were in ethnic evasion, a time when minorities adopt majority culture's negative views of the heritage culture and language, but as Feuerverger noted, it is possible that "promoting pride in cultural identity through encouraging first language proficiency, as in this specific intervention, the children's ambivalence about their culture can be overcome."

20. Feuerverger, 1989.

21. Hornberger, 1988, p. 251.

22. Brook, 1988, p. 105.

References

Acle, L., Jr. (1991, March 3). Platform: Bilingual education. *Los Angeles Times*, p. M7.

Arana-Ward, M. (1997, August 4). For children of the fields, education is elusive. *The Washington Post*, pp. A1, A9.

August, D., & García, E. E. (1988). *Language minority education in the United States: Research, policy, and practice*. Springfield, IL: C. C. Thomas.

Bartlett, K. J., & Vargas, F. O. (1991). *Literacy education for adult migrant farmworkers*. ERIC Digest (EDO-LE-91–05). Washington, DC: National Clearinghouse for Literacy Education.

Beason, T. (1997, September 1). Free ESL classes in demand on the Eastside: Immigrants prompting new need. *The Seattle Times*, p. B3.

Bialystock, E. (1987). Words as things: Development of word concept by bilingual children. *Studies in Second Language Acquisition, 9,* 133–140.

Blake, L., Lambert, W. E., Sidoti, N., & Wolfe, D. (1981). Students' views of intergroup tensions in Quebec: The effects of language immersion experience. *Canadian Journal of Behavioural Science, 13*(2), 144–160.

Boswell, T. D. (1998). Implications of demographic changes in Florida's public school population. In S. H. Fradd & O. Lee (Eds.), *Creating Florida's multilingual global work force: Educational policies and practices for students learning English as a new language* (pp. I-1–I-23). Tallahassee, FL: Florida Department of Education. (ERIC Document Reproduction Service No. ED 421 854)

Brisk, M. E. (1998). *Bilingual education: From compensatory to quality schooling*. Mahwah, NJ: Lawrence Erlbaum Assoc.

Brook, K. L. (1988). Language maintenance in the Japanese American community (Master's thesis, California State University, Long Beach, 1988). *Dissertation Abstracts International, 27–02,* AAI1335085.

California Department of Education. (1995). *Language census report for California public schools: 1995*. Sacramento: Author.

Calsamiglia, H., & Tusón, A. (1984). Use of languages and code-switching in groups of youth in a "barrio" of Barcelona: Communicative norms in spontaneous speech. *International Journal of the Sociology of Language, 47,* 105–121.

Cho, G., & Krashen, S. (1998). The negative consequences of heritage language loss and why we should care. In S. Krashen, L. Tse, & J. McQuillan (Eds.), *Heritage language development* (pp. 31–39). Culver City, CA: Language Education Associates.

Clark, B. E. (2000, March 20). Language lessons: Bilingual employees get their say in the marketplace. *The San Diego Union-Tribune*, p. C1.

Clines, F. X. (2000, February 7). Linguists find dialect a-flourishin' in Appalachia. *New York Times*, p. A12(1).

Crawford, J. (1991). *Bilingual education: History, politics, theory and practice* (2nd ed.). Los Angeles: Bilingual Education Services.

Crawford, J. (1992). *Hold your tongue: Bilingualism and the politics of "English only."* Reading, MA: Addison-Wesley.

Crawford, J. (1997). *Best evidence: Research foundations of the Bilingual Education Act.* Washington, DC: National Clearinghouse for Bilingual Education. Retrieved November 3, 1999, from the World Wide Web: http://www.ncbe.gwu.edu/ncbepubs/reports/bestevidence/index.htm#Contents

Crawford, J. (1999a). *Language legislation in the U.S.A.* Retrieved from the World Wide Web: http://ourworld.compuserve.com/homepages/JWCRAWFORD/langleg.htm

Crawford, J. (1999b). *Bilingual education: History, politics, theory, and practice* (4th ed.). Los Angeles: Bilingual Educational Services.

Crawford, J. (2000). Language politics in the United States: The paradox of bilingual education. In C. J. Ovando & P. McLaren (Eds.), *The politics of multiculturalism and bilingual education: Students and teachers caught in the cross fire* (pp. 106–125). Boston: McGraw-Hill.

Cummins, J. (1989). *Empowering minority students*. Sacramento, CA: CABE.

Cummins, J. (1993). Bilingualism and second language learning. *Annual Review of Applied Linguistics, 13,* 51–70.

Cummins, J. (1996). *Negotiating identities: Education for empowerment in a diverse society.* Ontario, CA: California Association for Bilingual Education.

Dicker, S. J. (1996). *Languages in America: A pluralist view.* Clevedon, England: Multilingual Matters.

Downing, B. T., Truitner, K., & Truitner, N. (1980). A Vietnamese English dialect. *Minnesota Working Papers in Linguistics and Philosophy of Language, 6,* 13–27.

Draper, J. B. (1989). Efforts to overcome crisis: A survey of teacher availability in the States. *Modern Language Journal, 73*(3), 264–278.

Draper, J. B., & Hicks, J. H. (1996). Foreign language enrollments in public second schools, fall 1994. *Foreign Language Annals, 29*(3), 304–306.

Driscoll, A. K. (1999). Risk of high school dropout among immigrant and native Hispanic youth. *International Migration Review, 33*(4), 0857–0875.

Elley, W. (1991). Acquiring literacy in a second language: The effect of book-based programs. *Language Learning, 41,* 375–411.

Elley, W. (1996). Lifting literacy levels in developing countries: Some implications from an IEA study. In V. Greaney (Ed.), *Promoting reading in developing countries: Views on making reading materials accessible to increase literacy levels* (pp. 39–54). Newark, DE: International Reading Association.

Espenshade, T., & Fu, H. (1997). An analysis of English-language proficiency among U.S. immigrants. *American Sociological Review, 62,* 288–305.

Evans, H. (1986, March 31). Melting pot—or salad bowl? *U.S. News & World Report,* p. 76.

Faltis, C. J., & Hudelson, S. J. (1998). *Bilingual education in elementary and secondary school communities: Toward understanding and caring.* Boston: Allyn and Bacon.

Fernandez, R. M., & Nielsen, F. (1986). Bilingualism and Hispanic scholastic achievement: Some baseline results. *Social Science Research, 15,* 43–70.

Feuerverger, G. (1989). Ethnolinguistic vitality of Italo-Canadian students in integrated and non-integrated heritage language programs in Toronto. *The Canadian Language Review, 46*(1), 50–72.

Feuerverger, G. (1994). A multicultural literacy intervention for minority language students. *Language and Education, 8*(3), 123–146.

Fisher, R. I. (1974). A study of non-intellectual attributes of children in first grade bilingual-bicultural program. *The Journal of Education Research, 67*(7), 323–328.

Fishman, J. (1966). *Language loyalty in the United States.* The Hague, the Netherlands: Mouton.

Fishman, J. (1990). Empirical explorations of two popular assumptions: Interpolity perspective on the relationships between linguistic heterogeneity, civil strife, and per capita gross national product. In G. Imhoff (Ed.), *Learning in two languages* (pp. 209–225). New Brunswick, NJ: Transaction.

Fishman, J., Cooper, R., & Rosenbaum, Y. (1977). English the world over: A factor in the creation of bilingualism today. In P. Hornby (Ed.), *Bilingualism: Psychological, social, and educational implications* (pp. 103–109). New York: Academic Press.

Fixman, C. S. (1990). The foreign language needs of U.S.-based corporations. *Annals of the American Academy of Political and Social Science, 511,* 25–46.

Friedenberg, J. E. (1995). *The vocational and language development of limited English proficient adults* (Information Series No. 363). Columbus: ERIC Clearinghouse on Adult, Career, and Vocational Education. (ERIC Document Reproduction Service No. ED 391 104)

García, O., & Otheguy, R. (1994). The value of speaking LOTE in US business. *Annals of the American Academy of Political and Social Science, 532,* 99–122.

Gardner, R. C., & Lambert, W. E. (1972). *Attitudes and motivation in second-language learning.* Rowley, MA: Newbury House.

Garrett, P., Griffiths, Y., James, C., & Scholfield, P. (1994). Use of the mother-tongue in second language classrooms: An experimental investigation of effects on the attitudes and writing performance of bilingual UK school-children. *Journal of Multilingual and Multicultural Development, 15*(5), 371–383.

Gass, S. M., & Selinker, L. (1994). *Second language acquisition: An introductory course.* Hillsdale, NJ: Lawrence Erlbaum Associates.

Geer, C. H. S. (1981). Korean Americans and ethnic heritage education: A case study in Western New York (Doctoral dissertation, State University of New York at Buffalo, 1981). *Dissertation Abstracts International, 42,* 3896.

Giles, H., & Byrne, J. L. (1982). An intergroup approach to second language acquisition. *Journal of Multilingual and Multicultural Development, 3,* 17–40.

Giles, H., Taylor, D., & Bourhis, R. (1977). Dimensions of Welsh identity. *European Journal of Social Psychology, 7,* 165–174.

Grant, L., & Rong, X. L. (1999). Gender, immigrant generation, ethnicity, and the schooling processes of youth. *Journal of Research and Development in Education, 33,* 15–26.

Greene, J. P. (1997). A meta-analysis of the Rossell and Baker review of bilingual education research. *Bilingual Research Journal 21*(2 & 3). Retrieved May 12, 2000, from the World Wide Web: http://brj.asu.edu/archives/23v21/abstract.html.

Gumperz, J. J. (1982). *Discourse strategies.* Cambridge: Cambridge University Press.

Hagan, J. M. (1994). *Deciding to be legal: A Maya community in Houston.* Philadelphia: Temple University Press.

Hawkins, J. N. (1995). Politics, education, and language policy: The case of Japanese language schools in Hawaii. In D. T. Nakanishi & T. Y. Nishida (Eds.), *The Asian American educational experience: A source book for teachers and students* (pp. 30–41). New York: Routledge.

Heller, M. (1992). The politics of codeswitching and language choice. *Journal of Multilingual and Multicultural Development, 13*(1 & 2), 123–142.

Hernandez-Chavez, E. (1993). Native language loss and its implications for revitalization of Spanish in Chicano communities. In B. Merino, H. Trueda, & F. Samaniego (Eds.), *Language and culture learning: Teaching Spanish to native speakers of Spanish* (pp. 58–74). Washington, DC: Falmer Press.

Hewitt, R. (1982). White adolescent Creole users and the politics of friendship. *Journal of Multilingual and Multicultural Development, 3*(3), 217–232.

Hinkel, E. (2000). Soviet immigrants in the United States. In S. L. McKay & S. C. Wong (Eds.), *New immigrants in the United States* (pp. 352–358). Cambridge: Cambridge University Press.

Hoffman, C. (1991). *An introduction to bilingualism.* New York: Longman.

Hornberger, N. H. (1988). Misbehaviour, punishment and put-down: Stress for Quechua children in school. *Language and Education, 2*(4), 239–253.

Hornberger, N. H. (1998). Language policy, language education, language rights: Indigenous, immigrant, and international perspectives. *Language and Society, 27,* 439–458.

International Trade Administration Tourism Industries. (1998). *Tlnet: La Cumbre presentation.* Retrieved February 3, 2000, from the World Wide Web: http://tinet.ita.doc.gov/view/lacumbre/index.html.

Introduction of bills and joint resolutions, 104th Cong., 1st Sess. (January, 9, 1995) (testimony of Senator Selby).

Kloss, H. (1971). Language rights of immigrant groups. *International Migration Review, 5,* 250–268.

Kondo, K. (1998). Social-psychological factors affecting language maintenance: Interviews with *Shin Nisei* university students in Hawaii. *Linguistics and Education, 9*(4), 369–408.

Krashen, S. (1985). *The input hypothesis: Issues and implications.* New York: Longman.

Krashen, S. (1993). *The power of reading.* Englewood, CO: Libraries Unlimited.

Krashen, S. (1996). *Under attack: The case against bilingual education.* Culver City, CA: Language Education Associates.

Krashen, S. (1998). Heritage language development: Some practical arguments.

In S. Krashen, L. Tse, & J. McQuillan (Eds.), *Heritage language development* (pp. 3–13). Culver City, CA: Language Education Associates.

Krashen, S., & McQuillan, J. (1995). Contrary to popular opinion: English language proficiency and school performance of speakers of other languages in the United States. *NABE News, 18*(6), 17–19.

Lambert, W. E. (1974). Culture and language as factors in learning and education. In A. Wolfgang (Ed.), *Education of immigrant children*. Toronto: Ontario Institute for Studies in Education.

Lambert, W. E., & Cazabon, M. (1994). *Students' views of the Amigos Program* (Report No. 11). Santa Cruz, CA: National Center for Research on Cultural Diversity and Second Language Learning.

Lambert, W. E., Giles, H., & Picard, O. (1974). Language attitudes in a French-American community. *Linguistics, 158*, 127–152.

Lamm, R. D. (1986, July 1). English comes first. *New York Times*, p. A23.

Landry, R., & Allard, R. (1991). Can schools promote additive bilingualism in minority group children? In L. Malavé & G. Duquette (Eds.), *Language, culture, and cognition: A collection of studies in first and second language acquisition* (pp. 198–231). Clevedon, England: Multilingual Matters.

The language is the melting pot. (1985, September 27). *New York Times*, p. A30.

Lapham, S. J. (1993, September). *We the people: Foreign born*. U.S. Bureau of the Census. Washington, DC: U.S. Department of Commerce.

Lee, C. S. (1979). *Asian American students speak out. Philip Jaisohn Memorial Papers No. 6*. Elkins Park, PA: Philip Jaisohn Memorial Foundation.

Lee, J. F. J. (1991). *Asian Americans: Oral histories of first to fourth generation Americans from China, the Philippines, Japan, India, the Pacific Islands, Vietnam, and Cambodia*. New York: New Press.

Legislation designating English the official language of the United States, 101st Cong., 1st Sess. (January, 19, 1989) (testimony of Senator Shumway).

Lopez, D. E. (1996). Language: Diversity and assimilation. In R. Waldinger & M. Bozorgmehr (Eds.), *Ethnic Los Angeles* (pp. 137–163). New York: Russell Sage Foundation.

López, M. G. (2000). The language situation of the Hmong, Khmer, and Laotian communities in the United States. In S. L. McKay & S. C. Wong (Eds.), *New immigrants in the United States* (pp. 232–262). Cambridge: Cambridge University Press.

MacArthur, E. K. (1993). *Language characteristics and schooling in the United States, a changing picture: 1979 and 1989*. Washington, DC: National Center for Educational Statistics.

Macías, R. (1998). *Summary report of the survey of the States' limited English proficient students and available educational programs and services, 1996–97*. Washington, DC: National Clearinghouse for Bilingual Education. Retrieved February 12, 2000, from the World Wide Web: http://www.ncbe.gwu.edu/ncbepubs/seareports/96–97/f3.htm

Macías, R., & Kelly, C. (1996). *Summary report of the survey of the States' limited English proficient students and available educational programs and services, 1994–1995*. Washington DC: U.S. Department of Education, National Clearinghouse for

Bilingual Education. Retrieved March 13, 1999, from the World Wide Web: http://www.ncbe.gwu.edu/ncbepubs/seareports/94–95/index.html

MacSwan, J. (1999). *A minimalist approach to intrasentential code switching.* New York: Garland.

Malakoff, M., & Hakuta, K. (1991). Translation skill and metalinguistic awareness in bilinguals. In E. Bialystock (Ed.), *Language processing in bilingual children* (pp. 141–166). Cambridge, UK: Cambridge University Press.

McManus, W., Gould, W., & Welch, F. (1983). Earnings of Hispanic men: The role of English language proficiency. *Journal of Labor Economics, 1,* 101–130.

McQuillan, J. (1994). Reading versus grammar: What students think is pleasurable for language acquisition. *Applied language learning, 5*(2), 95–100.

McQuillan, J. (1996). How should heritage languages be taught? The effects of a free voluntary reading program. *Foreign Language Annals, 29,* 56–72.

McQuillan, J. (1998a). Language minority students and public library use in the United States. *Public Library Quarterly, 17*(1), 49–52.

McQuillan, J. (1998b). The use of self-selected and free voluntary reading in heritage language programs: A review of research. In S. Krashen, L. Tse, & J. McQuillan (Eds.), *Heritage language development* (pp. 73–87). Culver City, CA: Language Education Associates.

McQuillan, J., & Tse, L. (1995). Child language brokering in linguistic minority communities: Effects on culture, cognition, and literacy. *Language and Education, 9*(3), 195–215.

McQuillan, J., & Tse, L. (1996). Does research matter? An analysis of media opinion on bilingual education, 1984–1994. *Bilingual Research Journal, 20*(1), 1–28.

Mitchell, D. E., Destino, T., & Karam, R. (1998). *Evaluation of English language development programs in the Santa Ana Unified School District: A report on data system reliability and statistical modeling of program impacts.* Riverside, CA: University of California, Riverside, California Educational Research Cooperative. Retrieved from the World Wide Web: http//cerc.ucr.educ./Archives/SantaAna/SAUSD1.html

Moll, L. C. (1992). Bilingual classroom studies and community analysis: Some recent trends. *Educational Researcher: Special Issue on Bilingual Education, 21*(2), 20–24.

Mouw, T., & Xie, Y. (1999). Bilingualism and the academic achievement of first- and second-generation Asian Americans: Accommodation with or without assimilation? *American Sociological Review, 64,* 232–252.

Muller, L. J., Penner, W. J., Blowers, T. A., Jones, J. P., & Mosychuk, H. (1976). Evaluation of a bilingual (English-Ukrainian) program. *Canadian Modern Language Review, 33*(4), 476–485.

Myers-Scotton, C. (1993). *Social motivations for code-switching: Evidence from Africa.* Oxford: Clarendon Press.

National Association of Latino Elected and Appointed Officials Education Fund and the Tomás Rivera Policy Institute. (1998). *America's newest voices: Colombians, Dominicans, Guatemalans, and Salvadorans in the United States examine their public policy needs.* Los Angeles: The National Association of Latino Elected and Appointed Officials Education Fund. Claremont/Austin: The Tomás Rivera Institute.

Nichols, M. (Director). (1980). *Gilda live* [Film]. (Available from Warner Brothers Studio, Los Angeles).

Nielsen, F., & Lerner, S. J. (1986). Language skills and school achievement of bilingual Hispanics. *Social Science Research, 15,* 209–240.

Nieto, S. (1996). *Affirming diversity: The sociopolitical context of multicultural education* (2nd ed.). White Plains, NY: Longman.

Norton, B. (2000a). *Identity and language learning: Gender, ethnicity and educational change.* Harlow, England: Longman/Pearson.

Norton, B. (2000b). Investment, acculturation, and language loss. In S. L. McKay & S. C. Wong (Eds.), *New immigrants in the United States* (pp. 443–461). Cambridge: Cambridge University Press.

Olsen, L. (1997). *An invisible crisis: The educational needs of Asian Pacific American youth.* New York: Asian Americans/Pacific Islanders in Philanthropy.

Orellana, M. F., Lam, W. S. E., & Meza, M. (2000, April 24–28). *Immigrant children as language brokers: Implications for literacy learning in school.* Paper presented at the Annual Meeting of the American Education Research Association, New Orleans, LA.

Padilla, A. M., & Sung, H. (1997). *Less-commonly taught languages in elementary and secondary schools in California: A final report. Foreign Language Assistance Act Program Evaluation Report.* Retrieved May 10, 1999, from the World Wide Web: http://www.stanford.edu/group/CFLP/research/flaap/flaap.html

Peal, E., & Lambert, W. E. (1962). The relation of bilingualism to intelligence. *Psychological Monographs, 76*(27), 1–23.

Pease-Alvarez, L., & Winsler, A. (1994). *Cuando el maestro no habla Español*: Children's bilingual language practices in the classroom. *TESOL Quarterly, 28,* 507–535.

Pedroza, A., Jr. (1998, January 25). I know what it takes to learn English [Letter to the editor]. *Orange County Register,* p. G3.

Phinney, J. S. (1991). Ethnic identity in adolescents and adults: Review of research. *Psychological Bulletin, 108*(3), 499–514.

Pilgreen, J., & Krashen, S. (1993). Sustained silent reading with English as a second language high school students: Impact on reading comprehension, reading frequency, and reading enjoyment. *School Library Media Quarterly, 22,* 21–23.

The President's Commission on Foreign Language and International Studies. (1980). Strength through wisdom: A critique of U.S. capability. A report to the president from the President's Commission on Foreign Language and International Studies. *Modern Language Journal, 64*(1), 9–57.

Proposing an amendment to the Constitution of the United States with regard to the English language, 98th Cong., 1st Sess. (September 21, 1983) (testimony of Senator Huddleston).

Porter, R. P. (1990). *Forked tongue: The politics of bilingual education.* New York: Basic Books.

Porter, R. P. (1990, April 22). Language trap: No English, no future. *The Washington Post,* p. B3.

Portes, A., & Hao, L. (1998). *E pluribus unum*: Bilingualism and loss of language in the second generation. *Sociology of Education, 71,* 269–294.

Portes, A., & Rumbaut, R. G. (1996). *Immigrant America: A portrait* (2nd ed.). Berkeley, CA: University of California Press.

Pucci, S. L. (1994). Supporting Spanish language literacy: Latino children and free reading resources in the schools. *Bilingual Research Journal, 18,* 67–82.

Pucci, S. L., & Ulanoff, S. H. (1996). Where are the books? *CATESOL Journal, 3,* 111–115.

Quintanilla, M. (1995, November 17). The great divide. *Los Angeles Times,* pp. E1–E7.

Reveron, D. (1998, November). "Spanglish" won't cut it. *Hispanic Business, 20*(10), 14, 16.

Rhodes, N. C., & Branaman, L. E. (1999). *Foreign language instruction in the United States: A national survey of elementary and secondary schools.* McHenry, IL: Delta Systems and the Center for Applied Linguistics.

Ricento, T. (1998). National language policy in the United States. In T. Ricento & B. Burnaby (Eds.), *Language and politics in the United States and Canada: Myths and realities* (pp. 85–112). Mahwah, NJ: Lawrence Erlbaum Associates.

Rodrigo, V. (1995). *Spanish Vocabulary Checklist for Intermediate Students.* Unpublished manuscript. University of Southern California.

Romaine, S. (1995). *Bilingualism.* Oxford: Blackwell.

Rong, X. L., & Preissle, J. (1998). *Educating immigrant students: What we need to know to meet the challenges.* Thousand Oaks, CA: Corwin Press.

Ruíz, R. (1984). Orientations in language planning. *NABE Journal, 8*(2), 15–34.

Rumbaut, R. G. (1995). The new Californians: Comparative research findings on the educational progress of children of immigrants. In R. Rumbaut & W. Cornelius (Eds.), *California's immigrant children: Theory, research, and implications for educational policy* (pp. 17–69). La Jolla, CA: University of San Diego, Center for U.S.-Mexican Studies.

Santa Ana S. O. (1993). The nature of the Chicano language setting and definition of Chicano English. *Hispanic Journal of the Behavioral Sciences, 15*(1), 3–35.

Schecter, S. R., & Bayley, R. (1997). Language socialization practices and cultural identity: Case studies of Mexican-descent families in California and Texas. *TESOL Quarterly, 31*(3), 513–541.

Schön, I., Hopkins, K., & Davis, W. A. (1982). The effects of books in Spanish and free reading time on Hispanic students' reading abilities and attitudes. *NABE Journal, 7,* 13–20.

Schön, I., Hopkins, K., & Vojir, C. (1984). The effects of Spanish reading emphasis on English and Spanish reading abilities of Hispanic high school students. *The Bilingual Review/La Revista Bilingue, 11,* 33–39.

Schön, I., Hopkins, K., & Vojir, C. (1985). The effects of special reading time in Spanish on the reading abilities and attitudes of Hispanic junior high school students. *Journal of Psycholinguistic Research, 14,* 57–65.

Simon, P. (1980). *The tongue-tied American.* New York: Continuum.

Smith, B. (1998, April 27). Bilingual education, immigrants, and rights [Letter to the editor]. *San Diego Union-Tribune,* p. B7.

Smith, F. (1998). *The book of learning and forgetting.* New York: Teachers College Press.

Soto, L. D. (1997). *Language, culture, and power: Bilingual families and the struggle for quality education.* Albany, NY: State University of New York Press.

Starr, S. F. (1994). Foreign languages on the campus: Room for improvement. *Annals of the American Academy of Political and Social Science, 532,* 138–148.

Statements on introduced bills and joint resolutions, 99th Cong., 1st Sess. (January 22, 1985) (testimony of Senator Symms).

Statements on introduced bills and joint resolutions, 100th Cong., 1st Sess. (January 6, 1987) (testimony of Senator Symms).

Statements on introduced bills and joint resolution, 103rd Cong., 1st Sess. (February 24, 1993) (testimony of Senator Shelby).

Tajfel, H., & Turner, J. C. (1979). An integrative theory of intergroup conflict. In W. C. Austin & S. Worchel (Eds.), *The social psychology of intergroup relations* (pp. 33–47). Monterey, CA: Books/Cole.

Taylor, D. M., Bassili, J. N., & Aboud, F. E. (1973). Dimensions of ethnic identity: An examination from Quebec. *Journal of Social Psychology, 89,* 185–192.

Thomas, L., & Cao, L. (1999). Language use in family and in society. *English Journal, 89*(1), 107–113.

Timm, L. A. (1993). Bilingual code-switching: An overview of research. In B. J. Merino, H. T. Trueba, & F. A. Samaniego (Eds.), *Language and culture in learning: Teaching Spanish to native speakers of Spanish* (pp. 94–112). Washington, DC: Falmer Press.

Tse, L. (1995). Language brokering among Latino adolescents: Prevalence, attitudes, and school performance. *Hispanic Journal of Behavioral Sciences, 17*(2), 180–193.

Tse, L. (1996). Language brokering in linguistic minority communities: The case of Chinese and Vietnamese students. *Bilingual Research Journal, 20*(3/4), 185–198.

Tse, L. (1997). Affecting affect: The impact of heritage language programs on student attitudes. *The Canadian Modern Language Review, 53*(4), 705–728.

Tse, L. (1998a). Seeing themselves through borrowed eyes: Asian Americans in ethnic ambivalence/evasion. *Multicultural Review, 7*(2), 28–30, 34.

Tse, L. (1998b). Ethnic identity formation and its implications for heritage language development. In S. Krashen, L. Tse, & J. McQuillan (Eds.), *Heritage language development* (pp. 15–29). Culver City, CA: Language Education Associates.

Tse, L. (1998c). *An examination of the relationship between ethnic identification and attitudes toward the ethnic language: Toward a developmental model.* Unpublished manuscript.

Tse, L. (2000). Student perceptions of foreign language study: A qualitative analysis of foreign language autobiographies. *Modern Language Journal, 84*(1), 69–84.

Tse, L. (in press). Resisting and reversing language shift: Language resilience among U.S. native biliterates. *Harvard Educational Review.*

Unz, R. K. (1997, October, 19). Bilingualism vs. bilingual education [Editorial]. *Los Angeles Times,* p. M6.

Unz, R., & Tuchman, G. M. (1997). *English language education children in public schools*. Retrieved February 2, 2000, from the World Wide Web: http://ourworld. compuserve.com/homepages/JWCRAWFORD/unztext.htm

U.S. Bureau of the Census. (1997). *Profile of the foreign-born population in the United States, 1997*. Retrieved May 25, 2000 from World Wide Web: http://www. census.gov/population/www/socdemo/foreign/foreign98.html

U.S. Bureau of the Census. (1997, March). *Current population survey*. Retrieved December 12, 1999 from the World Wide Web: http://www.bls.census.gov/ cps/pub/1997/for_born.htm

U.S. Bureau of the Census. (1999). *U.S. population*. Retrieved December 2, 1999, from the World Wide Web: http://www.census.gov

U.S. Bureau of the Census (2000, April 11). *Population estimates program*. Washington, DC: Population Division. Retrieved April 2, 2000, from the World Wide Web: http://www.census.gov/population/estimates/nation/nativity/ fbtab002.txt

U.S. Department of Education. (1998). *Adults' participation in work-related courses: 1994–95*. National Household Education Survey (NHES). Washington, DC: National Center for Education Statistics.

U.S. English. (1999). *Frequently asked questions*. Retrieved January 20, 1999, from the World Wide Web: http://www.us-english.org/faqs.htm

Valdés, G. (1992). The role of the foreign language teaching profession in maintaining non-English languages in the United States. In H. Byrnes (Ed.), *Languages for a multicultural world in transition, Northwest Conference on the Teaching of Foreign Languages* (pp. 29–71). Lincolnwood, IL: National Textbook.

Valdés, G. (1997). The teaching of Spanish to bilingual Spanish-speaking students: Outstanding issues and unanswered questions. In M. C. Colombi & F. X. Alarcón (Eds.), *La enseñanza del español a hispanolhablantes: Praxis y teoría* (pp. 8–44). Boston: Houghton Mifflin.

Valdés, G. (2000). Bilingualism and language use among Mexican Americans. In S. L. McKay & S. C. Wong (Eds.), *New immigrants in the United States* (pp. 99–136). Cambridge: Cambridge University Press.

Velázquez, L. C. (1994–1995). Addressing migrant farmworkers' perceptions of schooling, learning, and education. *Rural Educator, 16*(2), 32–36.

Veltman, C. (1983). *Language shift in the United States*. Berlin: Mouton.

Veltman, C. (2000). The American linguistic mosaic: Understanding language shift in the United States. In S. L. McKay & S. C. Wong (Eds.), *New immigrants in the United States* (pp. 58–93). Cambridge: Cambridge University Press.

Wagner, D. A., & Venezky, R. L. (1999). Adult literacy: The next generation. *Educational Researcher, 28*(1), 21–29.

Walker de Félix, J., & Peña, S. C. (1992). Return home: The effects of study in Mexico on bilingual teachers. *Hispania, 75*(3), 743–750.

Weinstein-Shr, G. (1994). From mountaintops to city streets: Literacy in Philadelphia's Hmong community. In B. J. Moss (Ed.), *Literacy across communities* (pp. 49–83). Cresskill, NJ: Hampton Press.

Wiley, T. G. (1996). *Literacy and language diversity in the United States*. McHenry, IL: Delta Systems and Center for Applied Linguistics.

Wiley, T. G., & Lukes, M. (1996). English-only and standard English ideologies in the U.S. *TESOL Quarterly, 30*(3), 511–535.

Will, G. F. (1985, July 8). In defense of the mother tongue. *Newsweek*, p. 78.

Willig, A.C. (1985). A meta-analysis of selected studies on the effectiveness of bilingual education. *Review of Educational Research, 55*(3), 269–317.

Winsler, A., Díaz, R. M., Espinosa, L., & Rodríguez, J. L. (1999). When learning a second language does not mean losing the first: Bilingual language development in low-income, Spanish-speaking children attending bilingual preschool. *Child Development, 70*(2), 349–362.

Wolfram, W., Temple Adger, C., & Christian, D. (1999). *Dialects in schools and communities*. Mahwah, NJ: Lawrence Erlbaum Associates.

Wong, S., & Lopez, M. G. (2000). English language learner of Chinese background: A portrait of diversity. In S. L. McKay & S. C. Wong (Eds.), *New immigrants in the United States* (pp. 263–305). Cambridge, MA: Cambridge University Press.

Wong Fillmore, L. (1991). When learning a second language means losing the first. *Early Childhood Research Quarterly, 6*, 323–346.

Xidis, A. S. (1993). The impact of Greek bilingual programs on the academic performance, language preservation, and ethnicity of Greek-American students: A case study of Chicago (Doctoral dissertation, Florida State University, 1993). *Dissertation Abstracts International, 54*, 416.

Yardley, J. (1994, October 24). The hard lessons of bilingual education. *The Washington Post*, p. B1.

Zentella, A. C. (1982). Code-switching and interactions among Puerto Rican children. In J. Amastae & L. Eliaas-Olivares (Eds.), *Spanish in the United States: Sociolinguistic aspects* (pp. 351–385). Cambridge: Cambridge University Press.

Zhou, M. (1999). Coming of age: The current situation of Asian American children. *Amerasia Journal, 25*(1), 1–27.

Zhou, M., & Bankston, C. L., III. (1994). Social capital and the adaptation of the second generation: The case of Vietnamese youth in New Orleans. *International Migration Review, 28*, 821–845.

Index

Aboud, F. E., 90n. 7
Accent-reduction courses, 28–29
Acle, Luis, Jr., 6–7, 77n. 17
Additive bilingualism, 43
Adult education programs, 25–27
After-school schools, 35–36
American Council on the Teaching of
    Foreign Languages (ACTFUL), 37, 55
Arana-Ward, M., 81n. 32
Assimilationism, 54
Au, Kathryn, x
August, D., 75n. 3

Bankston, C. L., 86n. 6
Bartlett, K. J., 81n. 30
Bassili, J. N., 90n. 7
Bayley, R., 83n. 14, 83n. 23, 85n. 32
Beason, T., 81n. 29
Bialystock, E., 86n. 5
Bilingual education, x
    heritage language development and, 71
    maintenance, 67
    need for, 72–73
    types of programs for, 35–37, 54–58
Bilingual Education Act of 1968, 6
Bilingualism
    additive, 43
    benefits of, 48–51
    confusing non-English speakers with
        bilinguals, 43
    through foreign-language programs, 54–
        56
    through heritage language programs, 56–
        58
    importance of, 50–51
    lack of bilingual teachers, 51
    political instability and, 2–3, 6
    as rare, 43
    subtractive, 31–32
Biliteracy, 23, 31–32, 71
Borrowing, 42
Boswell, Thomas D., 14, 15, 78n. 2, 86n. 7
Bourdieu, Pierre, x
Bourhis, R., 90n. 7
Branaman, L. E., 55–56
Brisk, M. E., 83n. 15
Brook, Kathy L., 67, 68, 83n. 17, 91n. 22
Byrne, J. L., 83n. 10, 90n. 4

California
    Basic Education Data System, 55
    Proposition 227, 1–2, 7
Calsamiglia, H., 85n. 31
Cao, L., 87n. 22
Carter, Jimmy, 49, 55–56, 59
Ceridian Performance Partners, 49
Chang, Chou, 25–26
Children of immigrants. *See also* Heritage
        language development; Immigrants
    academic performance among, 19–21
    English-language acquisition among, 12,
        17–19
    language brokering by, 23–24
    limited exposure to heritage language, 33–35
    limited opportunities to learn heritage
        language, 35–37
Cho, G., 87n. 21
Christian, D., 84–85n. 30
Clark, B. E., 86n. 10, 86–87n. 13–14
Clearinghouse on Adult, Career, and
        Vocational Education, 26
Clines, F. X., 84–85n. 30
Codeswitching, 41–42
Commission on Foreign-Languages and
        International Studies, 49
Community, influences on heritage language
        development, 39
Coolidge, Calvin, 59
Cooper, R., 87n. 15
Crawford, Jim, x, 75n. 1, 75n. 2, 75n. 3, 78–
        79n. 12, 86n. 8, 87–88n. 24
Cummins, J., 75n. 3, 77–78n. 20, 82n. 4,
        87n. 18
Cunningham, Kelly, 49

Defense Language Institute, 48–49, 50, 87n. 17
Destino, T., 83n. 14
Díaz, R. M., 83n. 14
Dicker, S. J., 75n. 3
Downing, B. T., 84n. 29
Draper, J. B., 87n. 20, 89n. 27
Driscoll, Ann K., 21, 78n. 11
Drop-out rates, 20–21

Educational background
    recognition of immigrant, 27
    speed of learning English and, 22

About the Author

Lucy Tse is an associate professor of education at California State University, Los Angeles. She is co-editor of the book *Heritage Language Development* and has published widely in the areas of second language acquisition, heritage language learning, and bilingualism and biliteracy.